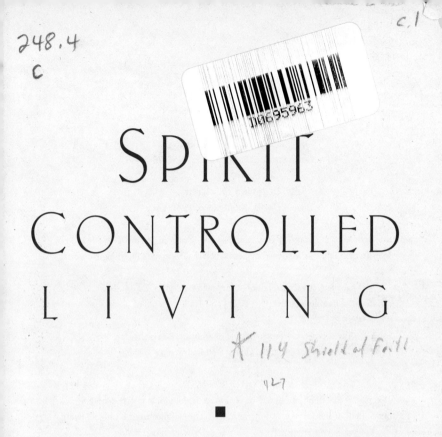

SPIRIT
CONTROLLED
LIVING

•

Clark Cothern

Multnomah Publishers® *Sisters, Oregon*

SPIRIT-CONTROLLED LIVING
published by Multnomah Publishers, Inc.

© 2000 by Clark Cothern
International Standard Book Number: 1-57673-639-3

Design by Chris Gilbert
Cover image by Kazuo Kawai/Photonica

Scripture quotations are from *The Holy Bible,* New International Version © 1973, 1984 by
International Bible Society, used by permission of Zondervan Publishing House

Multnomah is a trademark of Multnomah Publishers, Inc., and is
registered in the U.S. Patent and Trademark Office.

The colophon is a trademark of Multnomah Publishers, Inc.
Printed in the United States of America

For information:
MULTNOMAH PUBLISHERS, INC.
POST OFFICE BOX 1720
SISTERS, OREGON 97759

Library of Congress Cataloging-in-Publication Data
Cothern, Clark.
Spirit-controlled living: turning negative impulses into positive thoughts,
feelings, and actions / by Clark Cothern.
        p. cm.
ISBN 1-57673-639-3
1. Self-control—Religous aspects—Christianity.   I. Title.
BV4647.S39 C68 2000
248.4—dc21
        00-008305

00 01 02 03 04 05 06 07 — 10 9 8 7 6 5 4 3 2 1 0

To

KATHERYN FAYE COTHERN,

GAYLON CLARK COTHERN III,

and

CALLIE ELIZABETH COTHERN,

three walking, talking, loving,

learning examples of Spirit-controlled living.

You continue to teach as you learn.

Keep doing both.

Contents

Part One

Part Two

Acknowledgments

Thanks to each of you who were part of the team God put together to influence, encourage, inspire, motivate, kick in the pants, and love me through a painful-yet-wonderful growing phase of life called "the research and writing process."

Joy Cothern, author's wife, pastor's wife, professional mom, community servant, and the only one (besides the Lord) who *really* knows how much the author struggles with his own pesky impulses, quirks, and idiosyncrasies.

Trinity Baptist Church, a loving collection of sinners-turned-saints who continually amaze me with their desire to be obedient to Christ and their selfless prayer support as their pastor seeks to be obedient by writing.

Ed Gore, Ron Potter, Chris Pollard, and Frank Maguire, a hodgepodge of hilarious friends, accountability partners, and thought stimulators.

Joy Cothern and Carol Serafin, wives of the two guys who spent the most time on this thing and who each offered important insights from a woman's point of view.

Pat, Sue, and the rest of the gang at The Daily Grind, a place in Tecumseh, Michigan, where the best coffee in Lenawee County is served and where, at the back table, books are discussed and written.

Koby Marowelli and Beth Warren at The Image Gallery in Adrian, Michigan, specialist in taking off-the-wall nebulous ideas and turning them into understandable, visually incredible illustrations, graphs, charts, and graphics.

Dan Benson, Penny Whipps, Steve Curley, David Van Diest, Jeff Leeland, and everyone else at Multnomah Publishers, whose professional, ministry-minded fingerprints are all over this project.

Special Thanks

Joseph Serafin (MSW, DCSW) and his wife, Carol (MSW, DCSW), *are* Integrity Counseling. I figure Joe as the Brad character in this book. I'm more like Tom.

I got to know Joe when we worked together on a hectic and hilarious community nativity presentation for our town's Christmas parade. I could tell then that he was a highly creative, enthusiastic guy. I was delighted that a warm friendship grew out of that toe-freezing experience.

A couple of years later, I invited Joe to our church to teach a course on anger management to our men's group. He was definitely qualified, having worked for years in the field of clinical counseling and social work. He and Carol were running Integrity, a successful Christian counseling agency, and he was pursuing theological studies toward a master's degree.

While watching him work, the wheels began to turn in my head: *I'll bet some of the stuff he's using in his counseling and seminars would make a great book.*

Over the next few months, as Joe and I met together with a couple of other fun-loving, ministry-minded guys, Tom Hawkins and Doug Winters, I experienced once again the power of group dynamics and the supernatural support that emerges from strong friendships with fellow believers.

Joe graciously allowed me to shovel the idea of *Spirit-Controlled Living,* along with half a dozen other book ideas, into the "What about this one?" hopper, through which my editor, Dan Benson, and the capable marketing staff at Multnomah sifted.

Several ideas quickly ran through the little holes, but guess which one was big enough to remain? You guessed it. The idea for *this* book. In a phone conversation, Dan said, "I think *all* of us, at one time or another, struggle with impulses—big and small." He's right.

Joe readily agreed to let me systematically drain his brain. I don't know when I've had so much fun: pestering a professional Christian counselor, learning tons of new things, and then writing about them. In fact, Joe and I had *so* much fun that the other people in The Daily Grind, our favorite coffee shop and hideout for early morning meetings, probably thought we were just goofing off. A *lot* of laughter, a *lot* of effort and serious discussion, and a *lot* of coffee has been poured into this project.

The truth is, this book wouldn't be here if it weren't for Joe Serafin and his willingness to share years of insights and tools. I've tried to boil down his highly effective principles, add some spice, and roll them up in a tasty package so you or your study group can feast on the fruit of Joe's labor.

What I'm trying to say is, there's a *lot* of Joe Serafin in this book. Now I know why he and Carol are so sought after for counseling. They are both integrity incarnate.

Thanks, Joe, for your witty way of distilling complex concepts into crystal-clear, tasteful, bite-sized pieces. And thanks for revealing your heart, which is boiling from the fire of the Holy Spirit, filled to the brim with dedication to the Father's work, and running over with love for His Son, Jesus Christ.

It's an honor to call you friend.

Let's do this again sometime.

Part One

■

The first section of *Spirit-Controlled Living* takes you through a step-by-step biblical model for effective, Spirit-transformed impulse management. Using a fictional setting with a group of realistic composite characters, you can walk through the process by "sitting in" on the group's sessions. I think you'll find the group members very cordial—and that you'll readily identify with some of their personal struggles.

The impulse development model presented and the tools learned in part one will apply to practically any impulsive behavior you wish to conquer.

chapter one

EVEN NICE PEOPLE HAVE PESKY IMPULSES

What Impulse, Emotion, or Bad Habit Troubles *Your* Life?

Hon-n-n-n-k!

Tom slammed his palm on the horn to announce his strong disapproval of the Taurus's abrupt lane change. The driver of the silver car glanced back at Tom in his rearview mirror, then raised his hand to display a universally understood reply. Veins bulged in Tom's neck as he held his hand hard against the horn for a good five seconds. The snapshot of the driver's profile imprinted itself in his brain, and Tom memorized the oval-shaped, white patch of hair—a birthmark, he figured—which stood out like a searchlight on the right side of the young man's dark brown hair.

"You IDIOT!" he screamed—loudly enough to strain his

voice. But the driver of the Taurus heard nothing over the deafening roar of the construction machinery that had caused the lane closure.

Traffic crept along in random spurts ranging from five to fifteen miles an hour in the only lane still open. Tom's jaw clenched, and his knuckles blanched whiter on the wheel as he maneuvered the front bumper of his newly acquired Camry as close to the rear bumper of his newly acquired enemy as possible.

Then the clot of traffic broke up, and the culprit Taurus steered north as Tom headed east to his morning meeting. A thought formed in Tom's head as quickly as the traffic had dispersed: *Wouldn't it be embarrassing if that guy turned out to be the client I'm supposed to meet with today?*

He quickly dismissed the thought with a chuckle. *Nah. Wouldn't happen. He took off in another direction. I'll probably never see the jerk again.*

But then, he thought, *what if that guy shows up in my cell group this Friday? Now that would be a kick in the khakis, wouldn't it?*

Chuckling to himself, Tom began the final leg of his morning commute. *I'd sure feel silly facing that fellow, knowing that he had witnessed my little horn-honking concert. I'd hate to see the look on his face when he found out that I was his new Bible study teacher.*

Tom arrived at work with just enough time to check his hair in the restroom mirror before heading to the conference room to meet the young executives who had hired him to help sell their products. He secretly breathed a sigh of relief as he shook hands with each person in the room. *Whew,* he thought. *No circles of white hair.* Then, with a wry bit of humor to cover his nervousness, he asked, "None of you here drives a silver Taurus, do you?" Every head shook no. "Good! Let's get started."

His week was so busy that he totally forgot about the freeway incident until Friday evening. Only fifteen minutes into the Bible study, one of the cell group members read from Paul's letter to the Romans: "I do not understand what I do. For what I want to do I do not do, but what I hate to do" (Romans 7:15).

Tom addressed a discussion question to the group: "If you were to see yourself on videotape acting rudely toward someone else, how would you feel?" But he didn't listen very closely to the answers zigzagging around the room. He was thinking, *I'd feel pretty embarrassed. In fact, when I see anger in others, I hate it. So why is it that I can decide to act one way and then, someone pushes my button and, without even thinking, WHAM, I act another way?*

Before he could formulate an answer to his own question, another group member read ahead in the Scripture passage, "For what I do is not the good I want to do; no, the evil I do not want to do—this I keep on doing" (Romans 7:19).

Remembering his role as discussion leader, Tom asked the next question in his study guide: "Does it make you feel any better about yourselves to know that Paul was a man everyone respected, yet even he struggled with his impulsive tendencies?"

Heads nodded.

He listened to a few others offer their insights, but inwardly he was afraid they might detect the guilt he was feeling about his own hot temper, which had resulted in road rage earlier in the week. *What if they find out that I struggle with this stuff too? Will it undermine my leadership?*

After the meeting ended, Tom helped his wife carry coffee cups to the kitchen and continued the silent conversation with himself.

Sure, Paul had human tendencies, like the rest of us. That's a relief. It's comforting to know that the man we all think of as highly successful struggled with impulsive behavior. But even though I know Christ is the answer to my anger problem, I can't seem to get a grip on this one area. I need help.

That's when Tom remembered the flyer he had on his desk at work. It announced a course at nearby Trinity College on impulse control, taught by Brad, a friend of his from church.

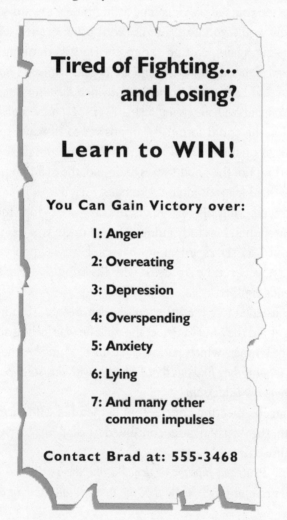

Tired of Fighting... and Losing?

Learn to WIN!

You Can Gain Victory over:

1: **Anger**

2: **Overeating**

3: **Depression**

4: **Overspending**

5: **Anxiety**

6: **Lying**

7: **And many other common impulses**

Contact Brad at: 555-3468

The next morning Tom called Brad in his counseling office. After some banter about the weather, he got to the point. "Brad, what I'm hoping to get out of the course is, *how* do I get a handle on my anger? I know what the Bible says about it, and I've heard all the typical Sunday school answers. But I still struggle with the impulse to run someone off the road when they cut me off, like a guy did the other day."

Brad responded, "You help sell things for people, right?"

"Yep."

"And to do that, you have to understand how people think and what motivates them to buy, right?"

"Right."

"Well, sometimes it helps to know what motivates us to do what we do, even when it comes to impulsive behavior like anger. Just knowing *how* something works makes it easier to know *how to fix it* when it's not working right."

"That makes sense."

"I think this course will help answer your questions. We're going to take twelve weeks, one session per week, to look at what motivates people to act on their impulses. With your sales experience and what you already know about the Bible, I think you'll do well in this course. And it will help you with other problems besides anger. You'll learn some techniques to help you allow the Holy Spirit to guide you when you are tempted to give in to your impulses. And Tom, I've heard you teach before. This is the kind of stuff you could use in one of your own small group studies."

"Sounds good. Count me in."

Dessert Dilemma

At the deli cash register, Kaycee eyed the rich, dark chocolate labeled Bodacious Brownies in the glass case. She sighed, then blinked away the image of herself devouring one of the delicious little cakes. The young lady behind the counter witnessed Kaycee's split-second moment of temptation. "They really are out of this world. And you can walk it off on the way back to the office."

"I don't know...." Kaycee hesitated. She looked around to see if anyone from the office was around.

"Aw, go on," the clerk prodded, "you owe it to yourself. Think of it as a reward for a job well done this week. After all, it's Friday."

"Okay," Kaycee said, feeling flushed with embarrassment and excitement. She knew she didn't need that dessert. *But since I'm only eating a salad for lunch, it will balance out.*

She smiled sheepishly as she pocketed her change and headed to the back table where, after scarfing her salad, she indulged in the delights of her favorite impulsive obsession and her most frustrating dieting downfall: chocolate.

On the two-block stroll back to the office, she thought, *Why do I always do that? I'm never going to lose that extra fifteen—okay, those twenty pounds—if I keep giving in.*

Her afternoon flew as phone calls and computer work made it easy for Kaycee to put her guilt on the back burner. It returned that evening when the topic in her cell group meeting turned to impulses.

She listened quietly as the discussion leader, Tom, responded to a passage they had just read. He said something like, "Does it make you feel any better about yourselves to know that Paul was a man everyone respected, yet even he struggled with his impulsive tendencies?"

As others in the group nodded their heads, Kaycee wrestled with the question. *Well, people respect me on the job and at home and even at church, but I'm not so sure I respect myself. I really need to take a bite out of those impulses instead of biting into more chocolate.*

We All Struggle with Impulses

It's time to do something about it.

Tom and Kaycee attended the same cell group meetings. They attended the same church. They had many of the same friends. Both were thought of as successful, motivated, accomplished, friendly, fun-loving people by their friends. Everyone they knew said great things about them: "They've really got it together." "They're great parents." "They are such good role models."

Yet both felt they could do better at curbing their impulses. Both had begun wondering, *What would people think of me if they knew what I struggle with?* They wanted to take control in those seemingly simple yet frustrating situations where impulses got the best of them.

Fortunately, Tom and Kaycee just happened to be married to each other. And they began to talk about their inner struggles with each other. It started the night after Tom signed up for the impulse management course.

"Honey," he began nervously, "are you asleep yet?"

"Yes," Kaycee said sleepily. But then she rolled over onto her back. "And I'm having a dream that my husband is talking to me in my sleep."

"I signed up for a college course. It's being taught by Brad. You know, from church?"

Kaycee got quiet. "Brad, the...*counselor?*" She shifted her gaze to the ceiling. "Is something wrong? I mean, you know, with us?"

"Oh, honey, no. Not at all. It's me. It's *my* problem. I just want to get a grip on my anger. I know I haven't told you much about how I feel, but I've been really angry at myself for getting so angry all the time."

"Let me get this straight," Kaycee said, relieved this conversation wasn't about her. "You are mad because you're mad?"

"Right. I'm tired of being Mr. Example to everyone else, but feeling like Mr. Failure to myself. Tonight during the Bible study, when we were talking about Paul and the struggle he had…well, that's how *I* feel. And I made a decision. I need to do something about my problem. You don't usually see it, but lately, I've been exploding more and more, especially at total strangers."

"You didn't yell at some old lady who had twelve items in the ten-item lane, did you?"

"No, no, nothing like that. I've just gotten so ticked off at those stupid drivers who cut me off, cutting in with inches to spare." His voice had escalated to a higher pitch, and his neck muscles had tensed. "Like that moron in a silver Taurus this week. You couldn't have slid a piece of paper between his rear bumper and my fender." Tom was sitting almost upright by now.

"Honey," Kaycee said in a velvety smooth voice, like a hypnotist talking to someone in a trance, "let it goooooooo." With her index finger she gently pushed on his forehead until he lay his head back onto his pillow.

He laughed and relaxed a little. "*That,* I'm afraid, is the problem. I don't know *how* to let it go. That's why I decided to take that course on impulse control at the college. It sounds like the kind of practical stuff I need to help me. And Brad's teaching it. I trust him. He's solid. I want to get some advice from someone who deals with this kind of thing."

"You're really serious about this, aren't you?"

Tom could tell she was concerned at how passionate he had become talking about his anger. "I mean," he said, "it's not like I'm going to turn into a serial killer or something...."

"I hope not. What would our kids do without their Frosted Flakes?"

"Ha, ha. I mean, I don't feel like I'm some nut case who needs a shrink, but I'm worried enough about this anger thing that I want to *do* something about it. So I signed up for the class."

"Can I make a confession to you?" Kaycee asked, suddenly serious. "The truth is, I was thinking about getting some help myself, but with me it's not about anger. It's—promise you won't laugh—chocolate."

Pause. "Chocolate?"

"Yes," she said. "I'd really like to lose a few pounds, but I just can't say no to it, you know? Desserts, snacks—I've gotta have my chocolate fix. It's like my body goes on autopilot and my mouth says yes even though my brain is saying no."

"Tell you what," he said.

"What?"

"Why don't I sign *you* up, too, and we can take this course together. That way, you can help me with my anger and I can help you with your chocolate. Whattaya say?"

"Hmm. Okay. Sounds good." She shook his hand. Then she leaned over, kissed him, and rolled back over onto her side. "Oh, and Tom?" she said over her shoulder.

"Yes?"

"If I hear you get up in the middle of the night, I'm checking the cereal in the pantry."

"And if I hear *you* get up, I'm hiding the chocolate."

chapter two

START WITH
YOUR PESKIEST
EMOTION

Learn to Gauge Its
Frequency and Intensity
in Your Life

S IX MONTHS LATER, in Tom and Kaycee's living room, where they have hosted an introductory cell group meeting on the topic of impulse control.

"So that's how Tom and I became interested in this topic," said Kaycee, wrapping up her opening remarks to the new group.

"And of course," Tom added, "since Kayc and I now have perfected our control over every area of *our* impulses, we'd like to share our expert advice with the rest of you."

Laughter all around.

"Actually, we would like to come clean and let you know," said Kaycee, "that we were surprised to discover how many people like us struggle with one or two annoying impulses that drive them crazy—even though the rest of their lives seem to be going along just fine."

Tom added, "So, with the permission of our counselor friend, Brad—the guy who taught the course we attended—we're going to share some things we've learned in our quest. We thought that our discoveries might just help others—like *you,* for example. Later in our study, Brad is going to join us for one session as our special guest teacher to present some material, answer questions, and correct all my teaching mistakes."

More laughter.

"Now," Tom said with let's-get-started authority, "you guys all met each other before, when you came to the interest meeting at church. That's what has brought us together. You each had an interest in our topic. But we should probably start by getting to know just a little about each one of you."

That was Kaycee's cue. She began passing out folded slips of paper. "When you arrived, each of you wrote the title of 'your song' from high school or college. Or at least *any* song you could recall from that long ago. Each of you is now holding the title of someone else's song. In just a moment, we're all going to walk around the room singing 'our song'—the one we wrote on our slip of paper. When the person who's been given your song title recognizes it, he'll say, 'Hey, I've got your song!' and write your name on the back of his slip of paper.

"Here's the tricky part—while you're singing *your* song, you also have to be listening for the song that's on the slip of paper I've given you. Got it?"

Some chuckled. Others groaned. Tom yelled "Go!" and the group sprang into organized chaos. Bits of familiar songs collided in midair as the group members milled about, trying to sing and listen at the same time. After five hilarious minutes, all the songs had been identified—with a little cheating from Vicki, who had walked around grabbing the slips of paper out of others' hands until she recognized her handwriting.

After everybody settled in their chairs, Tom wrote down each person's name and song title on a dry eraser board in front of the TV. Then he asked everybody to confess their age and occupation. The last person who spoke up was Sandi, the only African-American in the group. With a big smile she said, "Now, you've probably noticed that I happen to be different from the rest of you." She paused for effect. "I'm the only nurse in the bunch."

"Well, that's good to know," said Tom, writing her occupation on the board, "in case we work so hard that we need to be treated for exhaustion."

"And what about *you* two?" Sandi asked, referring to Tom and Kaycee. "We're not gonna let *you* off the hook. You two have to fess up about your ages, too."

So Tom added his and Kaycee's names and specs to the list. The board looked like this:

Our Group

Mike- the theme from James Bond
23, single, music store owner

Vicki- I Am Woman, Hear Me Roar
30-something, exec. secretary

Ron- Bye-Bye, Miss American Pie
50-ish, engineer

Sandi- Anticipation
37, nurse

Tom- If I Only Had A Brain
43, advertising/sales

Kaycee- The Lion Sleeps Tonight
41, "Professional Soccer Mom"

NOTE TO THE READER

■ After each new tool is introduced, you'll see an icon that looks like this:

Build a Skill

You'll get the most out of your study if you pause at that point and follow the accompanying "Build a Skill" directions to help you practice using the new tool you've just learned.

"Alrighty then," said Tom. "Now that we're all one big happy family, I'd like to introduce you to a helpful tool."

"Oh boy," exclaimed Mike, rubbing his hands together. "A power tool?"

Vicki looked over at Sandi and rolled her eyes.

"Well," Tom said, "I suppose you could say it's a power tool, of sorts. When you learn how to use it, you'll have more power over your impulses. In fact, you'll learn how to use several 'power' tools in the next few weeks. Each tool is pretty easy to use. If you learn to use one tool at a time, and practice with it, you'll develop skills that will change your life."

Vicki looked around behind her as though trying to find something and said, "Are we on camera? Are you shooting a commercial for this stuff, Tom?"

Tom began handing out a sheet titled *Hour-by-Hour Emotion Monitor Checksheet.*

Hour-by-Hour Emotion Monitor Checksheet

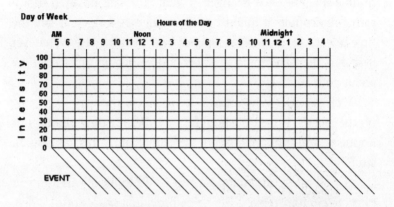

"Now," Tom said, "let me explain how this works. This worksheet will help you do some homework this week."

A collective groan—except for Ron, who said, "Oh, I just *love* homework."

"Teacher's pet," Vicki mumbled in a stage whisper.

Tom forged ahead. "You will each get to monitor your peskiest emotion—or urge—every hour for one week."

Eight eyebrows raised. Vicki huffed, "Every *hour?*"

"Yep," answered Tom, "and you're gonna *love* it! I guarantee. It might be a chore to start with, but after you've done it for a couple of days, this exercise begins to reveal things about you that you probably weren't even aware of. It's really very helpful."

Kaycee jumped in to support her husband. "The first time we got this assignment, I groaned too. But after about only three days, I began to see some patterns developing, and I was impressed with my insights into my own behavior. It was pretty neat."

"So here's how it works," Tom continued, ignoring all the comments flying around the room. "You don't have to worry about charting more than one emotion or urge if you don't want

27

to. All you have to do is figure out which one gives you the most trouble. For me, it was anger, so that's the one I started monitoring. For others it might be anxiety, depression, cynicism, the urge to eat, the urge to overspend, or something else. Whatever it is that keeps popping up *often* and causes you to feel guilty about your behavior."

Vicki asked, "Why are we doing this at the very beginning of the class? I mean, shouldn't we be learning about our impulses and emotions *before* we launch into this homework stuff?"

"Good question. I suppose you could think of this as a sort of pretest," Tom replied. "It helps provide a snapshot of where you are at the beginning of the course. Then, after you've learned some of the skills we'll teach you, you'll be able to see a positive change in your chart. It's always nice to have some measurable progress to keep you motivated."

Kaycee edged to the front of her chair, raised her hand high in the air, and like a first-grader with the right answer, exclaimed, "Ooh, *ooh!*"

Tom chuckled. "I can see I'm going to have my hands full. Yes, dear?"

"I think I have a story that helps explain how this tool can be useful."

Tom said, "Get your pens and pencils ready, class. This ought to be good."

"Well." Kaycee took a deep breath as though preparing to launch into a great discourse. "When I was about ten years old, my mother took me to get violin lessons at Mrs. Stephenson's house. She was really a kind lady.

"Anyway, on the very first day of my lessons, Mrs.

Stephenson pushed a couple of buttons on a tape recorder and told me not to worry about it. I didn't pay any attention to it since I was busy squeaking and squawking a few notes on my violin. I tried desperately to make any noise that sounded like music. After about five or six lessons, I was beginning to learn some basic scales, but I kept messing up the fingering on one of them. I got so frustrated that I plunked the violin down on my lap and said, 'I'll *never* be able to do this.' Mrs. Stephenson said, 'Oh really? Listen to this.' She reached over to her tape recorder and hit the play button. I heard these awful noises that sounded like fingernails on a chalkboard, and I asked my teacher, 'What's *that*?' She looked me straight in the eyes and said, 'That, my little Kaycee, is *you*, on your very first lesson. Remember?'"

Eyebrows lifted as lights went on in people's heads.

"I knew from listening to the tape of my squawks in that first lesson that I had really come a lot farther than I thought. I actually *had* improved! This motivated me to keep working hard because in comparison with my first lesson, I actually sounded pretty good. Well, maybe not pretty good. But better."

Sandi said, "Girl, you get fifty points for that story. Point taken."

Kaycee blushed and smiled.

Tom stared at his wife. "Kayc, we took that class *together* and you never told *me* that story."

"Well, you never asked!"

The group laughed again.

"Well, my amazing wife, who continues to surprise me even after these many years, has made a good point. After you have kept track of these urges for a few days, it's pretty incredible how you'll start to become aware of the triggers—those 'hot buttons' that tend to kick off the emotion or urge you struggle with most. Since we all tend to be creatures of habit, chances are that the triggers will all be fairly similar. I know when I started monitoring my anger, it surprised me how many of my triggers related to the same things. Like driving in heavy traffic, for instance. Once I realized how often I was getting upset in times like those, I was able to start doing something about it.

"But before I get ahead of myself, let me just encourage you to monitor your most frustrating emotion or urge for one week and then bring your checksheets back with you next week. I'll be honest with you: Those who take their homework seriously will get the most from this assignment and from the entire course. If you skip a few days or don't check your emotions at least every hour, you're bound to miss some of the red flags your own behaviors are waving for you."

Ron asked, "If we are aware of more than one emotion, would it be okay to go ahead and chart more than one?"

"I suppose so, Ron, if you're willing to go the extra mile. You could either do that by keeping a separate checksheet for each urge, or maybe you could devise a code and use a different symbol for each one to keep them apart."

Ron began jotting notes in the margin of his checksheet. "I can see the wheels turning," Tom said. "I can hardly wait to see what Ron brings back next week!"

Ron looked up from his notebook and flashed a sheepish grin at Vicki.

Vicki cocked her head to one side. "For the rest of us *way* down here where the *normal* people live, can you explain exactly *how* we're supposed to use this checksheet?"

"Sure, Vicki." Tom began handing out another version of the

checksheet, one with the word *example* plastered across the top. "All you have to do is take a brief 'time out' every hour and ask yourself how you're feeling. Kind of like a mental freeze-frame. Obviously, you don't have to wake up in the middle of the night to check how you've been feeling while you've been asleep."

Mike wiped his forehead. "Whew. That's a relief."

"You measure your emotional intensity using the scale along the left side of the checksheet. Consider it an 'intensity thermometer.' As you pause each hour, estimate where on the 'thermometer' your emotions or urges are at that moment. How intense is the emotion or urge you are charting? If you're fairly calm—say you estimate 20 degrees—then put a mark down near the bottom of the chart, across from the 20, in the square under the hour of the day you're checking yourself. See how the example shows a mark for each hour?"

Everyone nodded.

"If you are strongly experiencing the emotion or urge you have chosen to keep track of, then mark where you think it fits on the intensity scale. If you are *really* mad, or depressed, or fearful, or whatever you are monitoring, be honest and mark that hour way up on the scale."

Sandi interrupted. "Can we monitor overeating?"

Tom thought for a moment. "Sure, if that's your peskiest impulsive behavior. Hunger wouldn't really be considered an emotion, so that would fit more in the 'urge' category. And if that's your peskiest urge, then by all means monitor away."

Tom held up his example checksheet. "After a day, you should have a chart that looks something like this example, with marks all the way across the page, one mark for each hour. Are you with me?"

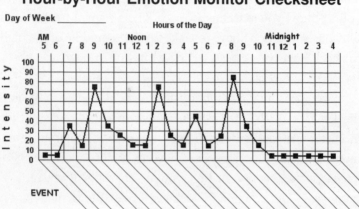

Hour-by-Hour Emotion Monitor Checksheet

Day of Week _____

Sandi yawned. "If you work a night shift, like I did last night at the hospital, are you allowed to chart sleepiness?" she asked.

She was joking, but Tom seized a teachable moment. "Believe it or not, that really can come in handy. Fatigue can often be related to other emotions, like depression or anger or irritability. So, yes, if you find yourself becoming overly tired much of the time, then you could choose to monitor that if you'd like."

Tom noticed a puzzled look on Vicki's face. "You look confused, Vick. Can I clear something up for you?"

"Yes. What if I get a certain urge three, four, or *five* times in one hour? Do I just average them all in and put one mark for the whole hour, or what? I mean, you guys should see what I have to put up with at work. I'll be honest with you, I get mad a lot!"

"Tell you what, Vicki," Tom said, sympathetically. "If you get angry several times in one hour, chances are that by the time you pause to check your emotion, you'll still be feeling quite angry. So just once an hour is okay for now.

"Oh, and do you see on your example sheets where there's a

place to write one or two words under each hour's column?"

The group checked their sheets and nodded yes.

"That's so you can write down a word or two to remind you of what was happening at that moment. For example, if you got mad because Joe told you to rewrite your report because it stinks, then maybe you would write *Joe* under the hour where you marked a 100 on your checksheet. Those little reminders will come in handy later as we start to recognize what pushes our hot buttons."

Tom nodded to Kaycee. "Hon, want to tell them what's next?"

Kaycee stood and announced, "The next item on our agenda is a field trip to the kitchen." She started to lead the way.

Sandi perked up. "Kitchen? As in dessert?"

Kaycee nodded.

Sandi hopped up to follow Kaycee. "You don't have to tell *me* twice. I'm there, honey!"

Build a Skill

■ Answer the following questions to help you nail down what you've just learned about using the *Hour-by-Hour Emotion Monitor Checksheet.*

1. How many emotions or urges should you concentrate on during the first week?

2. How often should you stop to do a freeze-frame and gauge your feelings?

3. When you stop to evaluate your emotion or urge, you are going to rate the_____ on the chart.

4. If you are fairly calm when you monitor your emotion or urge, where on the chart would you place a mark?

5. If your urge or emotion is quite intense at the time you check yourself, where on the chart would you place a mark?

6. At the bottom of the sheet, under each hour column, you will write a one- or two-word _____ of what was happening when you experienced the emotion or urge you are charting.

chapter three

HOW YOUR MEMORIES LEAD TO YOUR EMOTIONS

Understanding the Impulse Process

L et's quickly review," Tom said as the group's banter died down. "What did we learn from last week's homework assignment? Did everyone bring their checksheets?" Everyone answered yes, but Vicki appeared frustrated.

"You seem less than enthusiastic there, Vick."

"Well, with this monitoring tool, I discovered something good and something bad about myself," Vicki replied, scowling.

"Oh?" Tom asked.

"Yeah. The good thing is, I'm consistent. The bad thing is, I'm mad all the time!"

Tom probed a bit further. "Did you hit quite a few high spots on your chart?"

"Oh yeah," she said, holding up her checksheet. "If my graph were on a heart monitor, I'd be flat-lined."

"Well, don't forget about Kaycee's violin story," Tom said. "Now that you have a snapshot of where you are at the beginning of the course, it will be easier for you to see progress as you build new skills."

"I sure hope so."

"In fact, I wouldn't be at all surprised if in just a few weeks, you all see a marked difference. Ron, I've been curious to see what your chart looks like. Knowing your ability to learn a concept and improve on it, I expected you to bring a PowerPoint presentation to illustrate what you monitored last week. Or at least a stack of overheads."

Ron laughed and held up his checksheet. It had three symbols in each column: a triangle to represent anger, a circle for stress, and a square for fatigue. Using colored pens, he had drawn a color-coded map of his emotional ups and downs.

Most of the group reacted with positive comments and applause. Vicki, however, rolled her eyes. "There's always one overachiever in every class."

Ron shrugged. "I couldn't help noticing a connection between all three of these things. It seems that the stuff I labeled 'stress' almost always preceded anger. And following any episode in which I felt angry, I became really fatigued. That's why I started charting all three, since it became evident that I got really worn out after I felt angry."

"Interesting that you see those connections, Ron, because that's what I discovered about my own anger," Tom observed. "It seems that anger and depression are closely linked and often work together in a sort of cycle. Depression builds into anxiety or stress, and then if we express our anger, we often feel badly about our behavior and tend to slump back into depression again. It's quite common, according to Brad. But just so the rest of you won't feel too bad if your chart doesn't look like Ron's, all you had to chart this first week was *one* emotion or urge. So if that's what you've done, you're right on track. We'll add a new element each week as we build our skills. Ron's just a bit ahead of the game."

Vicki was waiting for Tom to pause so she could continue razzing Ron. "So Ron, I'll bet you *really* got angry. What was the worst thing you did, break a pencil?"

Ron smiled. "Actually, I sort of went on a garage-straightening rampage. I tend to work out my frustration by cleaning and organizing. It seems like such a productive way to burn up excess energy."

Vicki laughed and shook her head. "I should be so lucky."

Tom began to steer the group toward the evening's topic. "I'm glad you all did your homework. I give you each an A."

"And Ron gets an A plus," Vicki said.

"Now that we've learned something about our first tool, I'd like to paint for you a big picture of how impulses work." Tom distributed a handout titled *The Impulse Process*.

The Imp

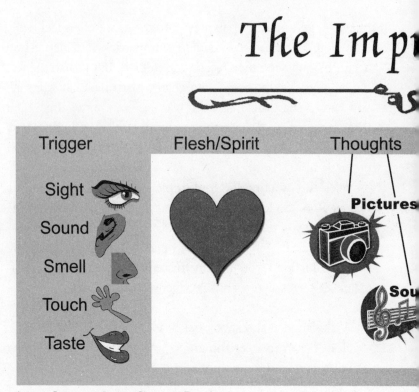

An Impulse Is a Process, Not a Thing

"You can see by the illustration that an impulse is not a *thing*. It's a *process*. Like fire, for example. Fire is a process, constantly growing, changing, or dying down."

Heads nodded in understanding.

"Now by looking at the chart, you can see that the process we call an impulse is divided into three stages: the Flesh/Spirit stage, the Thought stage, and the Feelings stage. All three stages work together to create that motivational inner urge we call an impulse. And though we're often not aware of it, this whole process can take place in a fraction of a second."

se Process

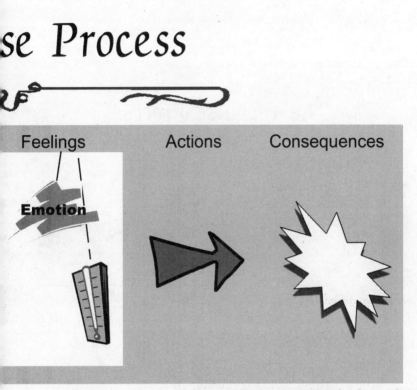

| Feelings | Actions | Consequences |

"Excuse me, Tom," Ron politely interrupted, "but what about that first column at the very left of the page. Did you miss a stage?"

"I should have known it would be the engineer who notices when I skip something. Actually, the first column is not a part of the impulse process itself. It represents the external stimulus that kicks off the whole shebang, putting the whole process in motion. Let me explain by asking a question. What does it take to start a fire?"

"A spark," answered Ron, who continued adding notes on extra pieces of graph paper he had organized into a three-ring binder.

"Right. And is the spark a fire?"

A couple of group members said no.

"Right. A spark by itself is not considered a fire. But is it the start of the process of a fire?"

Heads nodded yes.

The Impulse Process

Trigger	Flesh/Spirit	Thoughts	Feelings	Actions	Consequences
Sight		Pictures	Emotion		
Sound					
Smell					
Touch		Sound			
Taste					
Spark	Combustible Material	Oxygen	Heat	Flames	Results

Ron looked thoughtful. "Or like a spark that ignites gasoline inside a car engine, kicking off the whole process that makes your car move."

"Yeah. There you go. Good analogy."

Sandi grinned. "Fifty points to the man in the blue polo shirt."

Tom loved it when the group got this involved. "Though we've called it a 'trigger,' if it helps you to keep in mind the fire analogy, you could write the word *Spark* under the column with the heading titled *Trigger*. The spark triggers the whole internal process, which grows into an inner urge we call an impulse. So far so good?"

More positive head bobs.

"But before we get too far along, it's probably easiest to understand the concept of impulse development if we start right in the middle of the process, with the column called *Thoughts*. Once you understand where a thought comes from, how it's formed, and how you access it later, then the whole process, including the trigger—or spark—makes more sense. So, with that in mind, let me hand out *this* chart, which looks only at the *Thoughts* column."

Thoughts

Pictures

Thoughts Are Like Snapshots

"Let's think about thoughts for a moment. Let me ask you to think about your car. Someone describe for me the interior of your car—just the part you can see while you're sitting behind the wheel."

Ron looked around to make sure nobody else was about to speak. "The dashboard is dark gray, with an oval-shaped display in front of me," he began. "On the left side of the oval is a circular-shaped gauge—the tachometer—and on the right is another, matching circle—the speedometer. To the left of the steering wheel is a lever that operates the windshield wipers, and to the right is the shift lever. Cruise control settings are built into the wheel, and the logo of the car is embossed on the center of the steering wheel, behind which rests the airbag."

The whole group let out a collective whoa in response to Ron's detailed description.

"Now, Ron, how did you recall all that information?"

"I guess I was sort of looking at a picture in my mind."

"Excellent. That helps make my first point. Most thoughts are like a single snapshot—a picture in our mind's filing cabinet."

"Uh-oh," said Sandi, with an impish smile. "If my brain's filing cabinet is anything like the filing system at the hospital where I work, I'm in trouble."

"Well, Sandi, don't you worry," Tom said. He tapped his head with a finger. "If I can learn how to organize these snapshots in my noggin, then you'll have no trouble at all figuring out this stuff, I guarantee you. By the time you get through this study, you'll have your thoughts all cataloged in photo albums—all nicely labeled and ready to retrieve for practical application."

"Phew, I hope so," Sandi said, shaking her stylish cornrows from side to side.

"This snapshot represents a memory. Each memory is stored, like a picture, in a filing cabinet in your brain. Your memories are imprinted with an emotion—whatever you were feeling at the time your brain took the picture. That imprint is like a double exposure. You've got the original snapshot, and overlaid on top of that snapshot is an emotion. Does that make sense?"

They all nodded.

"Now, when you have a thought, your brain grabs a picture from its file. And because you are, as the psalmist said, 'Fearfully and wonderfully made' by your Creator, your brain inserts that single picture into a little movie clip, which you run very quickly to animate or give

Thoughts

Pictures

Motion Pictures

motion to the thought. Sort of like those little cartoon flip pages, where you see animation by flipping through the individual pictures real fast. It's a series of individual pictures that run together as a sequence to form a tiny moving picture. Still with me?"

"You bet," Vicki said as the others nodded.

"So, Ron, since you are able to retrieve such a clear snapshot of your car, can you pretend you are swiveling your head—panning your mind's camera, so to speak—from left to right and tell us what else you see inside your car?"

Ron stared straight ahead as though focusing on a picture suspended in midair. "Well, to my left, there is the door handle, with two toggle switches just above it. One operates the door locks and the other the window. Then there is the mirror adjustment knob. Panning past the dash equipment I described a moment ago, I can see the vents for the air conditioner, the glove box, and then the opposite door, which is a mirror image of the door on the driver's side."

"Excellent, Ron. Thanks," Tom said. "Now, what Ron just did was to grab a series of individual snapshots from his brain's filing cabinet. Then he flipped through them very quickly to animate a sequence, which became a short movie clip. He ran that sequence of pictures through his mind's movie projector, and what he saw as he described it to us was a tiny motion picture, as though he was moving his head from the left to the right side of the car.

"How about everyone else? Were you able to do the same thing with mental pictures of your own car?"

Most nodded.

Vicki spoke. "Tom, you said that our brains imprint an emotion along with the snapshot. Is that why a certain thought will cause us to feel a certain emotion?"

"That's exactly why. And in some cases, all it takes is a single thought, being played over and over again, like a movie clip that's been looped, to build the feeling's intensity. We'll talk about that in more detail when we get to that section on the chart. Good observation."

Vicki appeared slightly flustered, as though she wasn't quite sure how to accept the compliment Tom had just paid to her.

"Well," Tom launched into a recap, "let's review what we've discussed so far, to make sure we're all on the same page. Most of us tend to think in—" and he paused, holding an open palm to the group to solicit their response.

"Pictures," came the answer in unison.

"Right. And we then insert that single snapshot, or picture, into what?"

"A movie clip," someone answered.

"And we can play that clip over and over again, which then helps generate—"

"An emotion!" the group responded.

"Way to go, team," said Tom. "And Kayc, would you be willing to share what you learned from the course about what picture came to mind each time you charted the urge to eat? It might help if we hear from someone who has identified one of these through the charting process."

Kaycee blushed slightly. "Well, sure. You guys all know that I took the course in the first place to see if I could lose a little weight. Brad gave us the same homework assignment you guys did this past week. When I did it, I noticed—in the very first week—that every time my urge went way up in intensity, I happened to be at a place where they served really rich chocolate desserts. The two words I kept writing under each column when my urge would shoot up to the top of the scale were, *Saw chocolate*. I actually got to where I recognized the picture in my mind each time I got hungry. It was a picture of chocolate cake on a plate."

Sandi licked her lips. "Oh girl, I'm salivatin' already. Stop talking about chocolate before I go crazy."

Ron looked quizzical, but not wanting to interrupt the two ladies, he just raised his hand slightly. Tom nodded in his direction. Ron asked, "Under the *Thoughts* column, there are *two* words, *Pictures* and *Sounds*. Where do the sounds come in? I would assume the sounds are like a snapshot, but instead of a visual picture, the memory is like a sound bite. Am I on target?"

"Bull's-eye. It's true that most people think in pictures, but some tend to think in sounds, or sound *bites,* more than others. For example, you might be driving along the highway, flipping through the radio stations, when suddenly a song comes on that conjures up a memory. That sound triggers a memory, which is imprinted on the sound, and your brain loops it over and over again into a sound bite audio clip. The more you replay that audio clip, the stronger the accompanying feeling becomes."

Mike scooted to the edge of his seat. "Like when I hear the theme song from *Sesame Street,* I get all warm and fuzzy thinking about my preschool teacher, Miss Hartman." He sighed, placing his hands over his heart. "I wanted to marry her, but she didn't wait for me to grow up."

Vicki said, "Good thing, too. She'd still be waiting."

Mike grinned wickedly at Vicki.

"Mike, you are *so* weird," Vicki said. "But, you know, even though I think it's odd that you wanted to marry your preschool teacher, I actually understood that thing about the song bringing to mind a memory and a feeling."

"Okay," Tom said. "Now that you have a very basic understanding of how thoughts are formed, let me give you this week's homework assignment."

"Oh, how fun," Vicki moaned.

Ron couldn't resist another friendly jab. He clenched his fists, raised them in the air triumphantly, and exclaimed, "All *right!*" Vicki exhaled loudly and shook her head. Everyone's attention returned to Tom.

"You're going to use the same monitor checksheet you used last week, only this time you need to add one simple element. Every time you pause to monitor your urge or emotion, you're going to try to 'see' the picture that comes to your mind when your urge kicks in. Just stop, think for a moment, and try to recognize the picture that accompanies the urge. Just write down a one- or two-word reminder below each column, like Kaycee did when she saw the picture of chocolate cake each time her urge shot up. Got it?"

The group members jotted reminder notes to themselves in their notebooks.

"Okay," Tom stood and stretched. "We'll wind up this session and adjourn for some coffee and really healthy snacks." He glanced toward his wife. "No brownies for those whose impulse problem is related to chocolate." She giggled.

Sandi blurted, "What? No brownies this week? I'm leavin'. What kind of a party is this? No brownies. I can't believe it."

"And after we've fed our bodies, we'll head home. Then next

week, we'll come back and feed our minds with a look at the types of triggers that spark the impulse process. Deal?"

"Deal," everyone said. And they scrambled for the kitchen.

Build a Skill

■ Answering the following questions will help you nail down what you've just learned about the impulse process and how thoughts are formed.

1. An impulse is not a thing, it's a _____.

2. According to the *Impulse Process* chart, what are the three stages which make up the process we call an impulse?

3. The impulse, which becomes an inner urge motivating us to action, is almost always kicked into action by an external stimuli called a _____.

4. Some thoughts are also formed from sounds. Can you think of a song which brings to mind a thought from your past?

5. What thought-snapshot does that memory extract from your brain's filing cabinet?

BONUS EXERCISE (OPTIONAL)

■ Here's an additional exercise that will help you develop the ability to "see the picture" in your brain. This ability will come in handy later, when you learn to pause to see what snapshot was brought out of your brain's filing cabinet by a trigger. You can do this exercise individually or as a group.

1. Describe the front of your house or apartment. (Be aware that you are seeing a single picture in your head as you do so.)

2. Now, in your mind, walk into your home through the door you normally use. Describe what you see on the opposite wall. (Be aware that you are seeing another snapshot, this time in another location.)

3. Swivel your mind's "camera" to the left and right, and describe what you see on either side. (Be aware that you are still describing single pictures, but that you are linking the pictures together in a panning motion, taking in more than just a single wall.)

4. Now, in your mind, walk through your home, room by room, and describe what you see. (Be aware that you are seeing multiple pictures, run together like a movie clip. You are seeing in your mind what you would see if you walked through the house with a movie camera—with all the single pictures linked together to form a moving picture.)

chapter four

WHAT MAKES YOU ACT THE WAY YOU DO?

Learning to Identify Your Personal Triggers

I'm fighting the impulse to blow a whistle to get your attention." It was Tom's friendly way of calling to order the evening's session. As the group's banter died down he passed around new handouts and asked, "Were you successful with the homework assignment from last week? Did you see some of those pictures associated with the urge or emotion you were monitoring?"

Mike volunteered, "Yeah. Each time I got the urge to ask a pretty girl out, I saw a picture of my preschool teacher."

"Oh boy." Vicki smiled and rolled her eyes. "Here we go again with the preschool teacher."

"Are you joking, Mike, or did you really see a picture that jogged your memory when you thought about asking someone out?" Tom asked.

"No, I'm not joking. I really did see her picture in my mind whenever I thought about working up enough courage to ask someone for a date. Seriously."

"From what you told us before," Tom said, "it sounds like that particular person must have treated you in a way that left you with strong, positive feelings."

"She did. I felt safe around her—like I could talk to her without getting all mealy-mouthed," said Mike.

"Mealy-mouthed?" asked Vicki.

"Yeah, you know, when you want to talk with someone and act really smooth and everything comes out all muddled up. Mealy-mouthed."

"Mike," Tom said, "you should keep track of that connection between the positive feelings you experienced with your preschool teacher and your feelings of anxiety when you think about asking someone out. Why don't you keep track of those two connected feelings as you continue to monitor your urges and feelings? As you learn some additional tools, you should be able to learn to recognize the triggers for those feelings—and they are probably linked to those feelings you had when you were in preschool."

"Okay," Mike said, looking slightly embarrassed. "I will."

Recognizing External Triggers

Tom gave him a thumbs-up to let him know he had done well to make the connection and then held up his copy of the hand-out they had just received. "Now, gang, see the five types of external triggers on this list? Notice something familiar about the five categories?"

Types of External Triggers

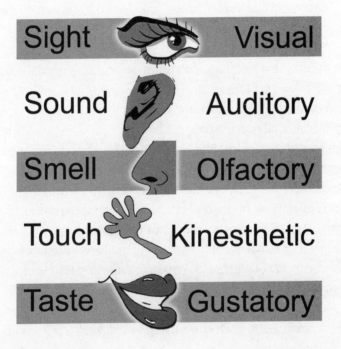

Sight	Visual
Sound	Auditory
Smell	Olfactory
Touch	Kinesthetic
Taste	Gustatory

Ron spoke as he scribbled some notes. "Well, they all relate to our five senses."

Tom lifted both hands high into the air. "Right. Our bodies are created in such a way that external stimuli are gathered through our five senses. Look at the list: *Sight*, or visual triggers; *Sound*, or auditory; *Smell*, or olfactory; *Touch*, or kinesthetic; and *Taste*, or gustatory. I love those words, *olfactory* and *gustatory*.

Use them tomorrow at work and amaze your friends. You could say, 'Wow, that coffee stimulates my olfactory and gustatory triggers, causing my brain to extract a snapshot from my cerebral filing cabinet. I think I'll insert that picture into a movie clip, play it over and over again, and increase the intensity of an imprinted emotion.'"

"Sure—amaze your friends," said Vicki, "then watch them haul you away."

"Now, remembering that a trigger is like a spark that ignites the process that develops into an impulse, can someone name for me one type of visual or *sight* trigger?"

Mike spoke up, this time with his macho bravado intact. "An athletic, tanned woman in a bikini."

"Don't hold back, Mike. Tell us what's *really* on your mind," Tom chuckled. "That, by the way, is *just* the kind of response we would expect from the youngest male member of our group. But it's true. The kind of person Mike just described *could* be a visual trigger. And, according to our friend Brad, men *are* usually more affected by visual stimuli than women. How about for you ladies? Are any of you brave enough to offer an example of visual stimuli? Something that triggers an impulsive response?"

Vicki spoke up in her most sophisticated businesslike tone. "We women are in such control that visual stimuli doesn't affect us as it does men."

Sandi blurted out, "Speak for yourself, honey. I get the urge to gain five pounds just by *lookin'* at those fancy dessert pictures in *Good Housekeeping*."

The ice was broken. The group was now definitely interested in looking at the various types of triggers that can kick off the process known as an "impulse."

■ Pause here and take a good look at the *Types of External Triggers* chart. If you are reading by yourself, write your answers in the spaces provided. If you are in a group, allow each willing participant to describe at least one type of trigger. Make sure you provide at least one example for each of the five categories.

Build a Skill

1. Sight (Visual)

   _____

2. Sound (Auditory)

   _____

3. Smell (Olfactory)

   _____

4. Touch (Kinesthetic)

   _____

5. Taste (Gustatory)

   _____

Recognizing Internal Triggers

After the group had come up with several examples of external triggers, Tom passed out another handout.

"Now let's look at internal triggers we all have. I place before you our next chart, fittingly titled *Types of Triggers*."

"You always come up with such original titles for these charts," Mike said.

"Well, I try. I suspect, based on the way Ron's been taking notes, that by the time he gets done with this course, he will have developed a CD-Rom on the subject, complete with computer-generated video examples and a fully-orchestrated soundtrack composed by John Williams and performed by the London Philharmonic. Ron, feel free to improve on my handout titles, okay?"

Ron grinned. "I have been."

"Fair enough," said Tom, holding up his newest chart. "Now, let's shift our focus from external triggers, which, by the way, bombard our brains through our five what?"

"Senses."

"Right. Look at the list below the circle that says *Internal*."

"As you'll see, these triggers are all based on our *physiological* needs—things that drive us as part of the way God created us to function. Notice, too, that the internal triggers at the top are needs which become quite intense, and very quickly.

THE NEED TO BREATHE

"Right at the top is our need to breathe," Tom pointed out. "Why is that?"

"Because without oxygen, honey, you'll be deader than a toad on a road in a huge hurry," answered Sandi.

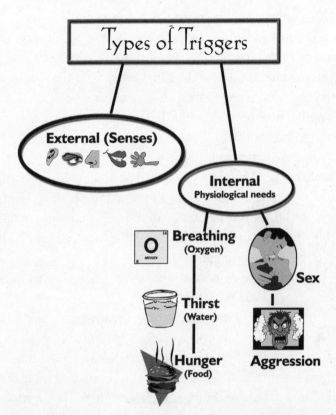

"Fifty points to the lovely lady in the corner. Now, Sandi, if we can just get you to come out of your shell and speak up."

Sandi put a hand on each cheek and tipped her head as if to say, *I know. I'm so shy.*

Tom asked, "Does anyone happen to know how long we can go without air before we cease to exist?"

Sandi jumped in: "Between two and three minutes before blacking out, between seven and ten minutes before significant brain damage occurs, unless you happen to be in ice-cold water at the time, and usually between ten and thirty minutes before you're headed to the morgue."

"Nice to have a nurse among us," Kaycee said.

"So, you suddenly have a severe asthma attack, and the intensity of this inner need is accelerating fast. What's going to happen to your thoughts and feelings when your three-year-old comes up to you trying to get you to read her a book?"

"Well, I'm sure not gonna be thinkin' about readin' no book," replied Sandi.

"You can say that again. And what else?"

Vicki spoke. "I suppose you would be thinking about getting your inhaler, if you had one, or getting to the phone to call for help, if the attack was *that* serious. And being a mom, I would probably be worried about who was going to watch my child if I had to get to the hospital."

"I'm sure you're right. And what about *feelings?* What might you be feeling, Vicki?"

"Hmm. Probably fear. Maybe urgency, anxiety—panic?"

"Absolutely. And as you can tell, when your physiological need gets really high, it's extremely difficult to concentrate on anything else. All you can focus on is meeting that immediate need. Can you see how our inner triggers add to the urgency of the moment? And how the higher the intensity of the inner trigger, the more drastic will be the feelings when an external trigger hits?"

Heads nodded.

THE NEED FOR WATER

"Let's briefly look at some of the other internal triggers. What about our need for water?"

"I'm all for it," Mike wisecracked. "You're supposed to drink at least eight glasses every day. Right, Nurse Sandi?"

"You go, my man," said Sandi. "Flushes the toxins, you know."

Tom wrestled to bring the group back. "What I *meant* to ask," he said,"was how long can we go *without* water?"

They all looked toward Sandi.

"Don't look at *me*. I'm not going to answer *all* the medical questions."

"About three days, I think," said Vicki.

The Need for Food

"Good," said Tom. "And what about hunger? How long can we go without food?"

"About fifteen minutes," Sandi said.

Vicki said. "I seem to remember reading that we can go for around forty days before we really begin to see ill effects."

"Well, it's quite obvious why God created the inner urges to breathe, drink, and eat. We need those urges to keep us alive. Looking ahead, though, I don't believe I'm going to even *ask* how long we can go without the next item."

The Need for Sex

For this topic, Tom went into lecture mode. "The need for sex seems to be built into the natural framework of who we are. God created us with all these inner needs for practical reasons, including the need for sex. Obviously, sex is necessary to propagate the earth and produce children, which is a way for us to contribute to society even after we're gone. And sex is given to us as a pleasurable kind of intimacy within marriage. But like all basic drives, if they become uncontrolled, sexual urges lead to behavior that becomes harmful. That's why God created boundaries. He loves us enough to keep us safe from the harm He knows will come to those who abuse His gifts."

Tom paused, checked his notes, and fanned himself with his papers. "Moving right along...."

THE NEED FOR AGGRESSION

"Can someone think of a positive reason why God created aggression as an inner urge?"

"For one thing," Ron offered, "aggression is necessary for a defense against danger."

"And it sure would come in handy to act aggressively if your child ran out into the street," Vicki added. "You'd need to act fast to keep him from getting hurt."

"Good," said Tom. "Aggression is a positive inner urge, given to us by God for good reasons. But what happens when we let our aggression get out of control?"

"People get hurt," Vicki said. "Look at all the killings we see on the news. That's an example of aggression that goes *way* outside God's boundaries."

"Good example," Tom replied. "I think I shared with you my own experience with road rage. I allowed my urge to get to a meeting on time, which in itself is a positive thing, to turn into unhealthy aggression and anger when another driver cut me off on the freeway. Anyone identify?"

Everyone smiled and nodded agreement.

Tom looked at his watch, then started one more stack of handouts around the circle. "One more graph to help us wrap up tonight's session. This one's called a *Topographical Needs Map.*"

Topographical Needs Map

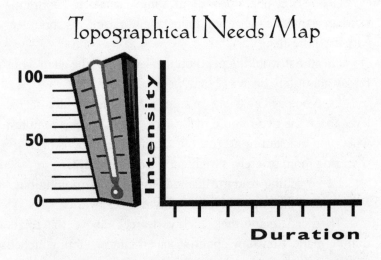

"The vertical line at the left of the graph is the axis labeled *Intensity.* The thermometer beside it illustrates how, when a need becomes great, the intensity goes up. The horizontal axis, marked *Duration,* measures a unit of time."

"Like minutes, hours, days, or weeks?" Ron asked.

"Right. Just to get an idea of how this graph works, let's use that asthma attack we talked about earlier as our example. Let's say that each one of those little marks along the *Duration* axis stands for one minute. Before an attack, both the intensity and duration are at zero. But suddenly, things are *not* normal; you feel an attack coming on. At one minute (or one mark to the right), when you are starting to wheeze, how high on the *Intensity* thermometer would we be? Just estimate."

"How about twenty degrees?" Kaycee said. "Because if you had asthma and knew what it was like, you might not be terribly worried right away, since you were accustomed to dealing with attacks."

"Good. How about *two* minutes into the attack?" Tom imitated an asthmatic, wheezing more visibly, raising his shoulders with each breath.

"I'm sure it would depend on the severity of the attack, but I'd say about fifty degrees," said Vicki.

"Everyone agree? Okay, let's put a mark at the fifty-degree level above the two-minute mark. How about at *three* minutes, when you are starting to run out of air?" He demonstrated by wheezing more severely, a frightened look in his eyes.

"I'd be getting ready to panic if my air was running out," Mike said. "I'd be up to at least eighty degrees by then."

"Then let's mark that. Eighty degrees, above the three-minute mark. And how about at *four* minutes?" Tom clutched his chest, not breathing at all.

Sandi shifted to the edge of her seat. "Brothers and sisters, I'd be prayin' the Lord's Prayer, recitin' the Twenty-third Psalm, and dialin' 911 all at the same time. I'd be blowin' the top off my thermometer!"

"In other words, you're at one hundred degrees' intensity at four minutes." Tom made another mark on his graph. "Now, let's play Connect the Dots and see what the topographical map of our internal trigger, asthma, looks like." He drew a line between his marks and held it up for everyone to see.

"Does everyone's graph look something like this?" The connected dots angled up sharply.

Everyone compared their graphs to Tom's and nodded.

"When the intensity of our internal trigger goes way up, it consumes our thoughts to the point where we can't really concentrate on anything else. As we move on through the impulse-development process in the next couple of weeks, you'll continue to monitor your feelings. You'll become really good at

Topographical Needs Map
Asthma Attack

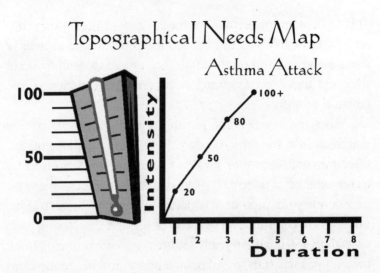

identifying your triggers, both external *and* internal. When you can learn to spot them right away, you can figure out why you're reacting to other people in certain ways.

"By becoming more aware of what's going on with these God-given impulses, you'll be in a *much* better position to allow the Holy Spirit to control the whole process. Hang in there through these early stages of learning, and in just a couple of weeks you'll be amazed at how the Spirit will start working in your thoughts, feelings, and actions."

"It really does work," Kaycee said. "You'll see."

Tom put down his chart and began the wrap-up. "Well, I have one more item to add to your Monitor Checksheet for this week's homework assignment." He paused, waiting for some protest. Everyone sat with pens in hand, ready for instructions.

"What?" Tom asked, surprised. "No whining tonight?"

Vicki grinned. "We've resigned ourselves. Just give it to us and get it over with."

"Okay. You've already done the checksheet for two weeks.

This week, continue to monitor the emotion or urge you've chosen. And just like you did last week, keep rating the intensity levels each hour and put down a word or two to remind you of the event that was transpiring at the time you experienced the emotion or urge.

"Also, try to access the picture in your brain—the picture you think of at the time you do your freeze-frame moment. But this time, start becoming aware of your triggers. Keep track of either external or internal triggers that are happening when you experience your urge or emotion. Write down those triggers under each column. You've been doing the monitoring long enough that you will probably start to see some patterns. I think some of you will start to make some pretty amazing connections between your specific triggers and the urge or emotion you are struggling with."

He paused again. The only sound was that of people writing notes.

"All clear on your homework?"

Heads nodded.

"I'm sorry," Mike said, shifting in his chair, "but I've got an internal trigger going right now. That coffee I drank has me at about an eighty on the intensity scale."

Everyone laughed, and a couple of them agreed. "Good example," someone said. "Makes it difficult to concentrate on much else, huh?"

"Thanks. Now can I go?" With that, Mike hopped to his feet and made a quick departure down the hall.

The meeting was over.

Build a Skill

■ To help nail down what you've just learned about external and internal triggers, complete the following statements.

1. External triggers are related to your five

   _____.

2. When an external trigger bombards your brain (through one of the five things you just mentioned above), it causes you to see a

   _____.

3. An internal trigger is related to a physiological

   _____.

4. A trigger can cause you to have a thought, which you can then run in sequence like a motion

   _____.

5. When a physiological need increases in intensity, your ability to concentrate on things around you

   _____.

chapter five

FEARFULLY AND WONDERFULLY MADE

Learning to Recognize Your Personal Body Cues

T om cleared his throat.

"I was going to start this evening's session by singing the song, 'Feelings,'" he said. "However…"

"By popular demand, you decided not to." Vicki finished Tom's statement.

"You're right. I don't want to drive you good folks away from our study."

"Oh now, honey," said Kaycee, "your singing sounds really wonderful in the shower."

"Well, thank you, dear," said Tom. "And that's about the only place it sounds wonderful. But I've got something much better than a song for you tonight."

"Brownies?" Sandi rubbed her hands together.

"Ha. Nope. Sorry, no brownies. Better. A new chart! Aren't you excited?"

"We can't wait," Vicki said.

"I knew you'd be thrilled." Tom started a stack of handouts around the circle. "When I first started learning about how thoughts, feelings, and emotions are all linked, I was pleasantly surprised to discover that many people really have a hard time identifying what they are feeling at any given moment. According to Brad, many of our feelings get all jumbled together, like different kinds of meats in a grinder, and it's hard to tell them apart. With me, emotions like anxiety, fear, and embarrassment would get ground together and come out as anger. Until I learned to recognize what different feelings felt like, I didn't know how to react to each of them. I just squeezed them all together, and they came out as my all-purpose emotion."

Vicki said, "That must be *my* all-purpose emotion too, then. But at least I'm consistent. I'm mad all the time."

The others laughed and nodded.

Tom continued, "One reason I had trouble identifying individual feelings is because I grew up in a home where feelings weren't openly displayed. I learned from my parents not to show my emotions, to shove them down under the surface. But I got frustrated because the more I buried my emotions, the more they jumped out at me at times when I couldn't really understand what was causing them.

"But I learned—and I'm *still* learning—that feelings don't have to be scary or 'bad.' And there are some fairly simple skills you can develop that will help you identify them. We're not talking rocket science either. This stuff isn't that hard to learn."

Ron looked pensive. "If you'll excuse me for just a second, Tom, I can't help noticing that we've skipped a step in the whole process. Can you tell us when we'll get to the phase on the *Impulse Process* chart called *Flesh/Spirit?*"

"Ah, yes. I should have told you that *before* we started this phase. I asked Brad the same question when he was taking Kaycee and me through this material. By learning first how the impulse process works, it's much easier to understand the Flesh/Spirit stage when we get to it. Once you learn the whole process, you'll see how, in the Flesh/Spirit stage, you can break out of a downward spiral of negative thoughts, feelings, and actions, and cooperate with the Holy Spirit as He redirects the whole process toward *positive* thoughts, feelings, and actions. It's in the Flesh/Spirit stage of the impulse development process that the real transformation begins."

"Okay," Ron said. "I thought there was a method in your madness, but I just thought I'd ask."

"No problem. I'm sure others were thinking the same thing."

"Yeah," Vicki offered, "but we're so used to your madness we didn't even question the method."

"Uh, thanks. I *think,*" Tom said, smiling. "Anyway, we're going to base tonight's discussion on what we learned last time about internal triggers. Remember when we graphed the asthma attack?"

Everyone nodded.

"We're going to use the Emotion Thermometer in a similar fashion. We're going to learn how to identify some *internal and external cues* that will tip us off when an emotion or urge is starting to get the better of us."

The Emotion Thermometer

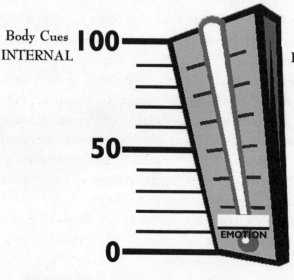

Kaycee spoke up. "Honey, maybe you should explain the term *cues*, or maybe give a couple of illustrations. When we took the class, I didn't really understand what Brad meant until he gave some examples."

"Yeah," Sandi agreed. "Whatchu talkin' 'bout?"

Tom chuckled. "Well, let's take the internal cues first. An internal cue can be any physical reaction that takes place when you experience an emotion. They may be cues to you, but not necessarily to those around you, because they are happening inside. For example, when I started charting my anger, I found out that my stomach starts to tighten up. At lower levels of anger, I can literally feel my stomach start to knot before the rest of the cues start to make themselves known."

Kaycee offered another example. "And when I'm starting to

feel tense or anxious, I can feel a heaviness in my chest, like it's becoming harder to breathe."

"Other internal body cues could be clenching your teeth or your fists, or maybe a slight headache, or changes in your breathing. Stuff like that."

"Or maybe like sweaty palms when you see someone *really* good looking?" Mike asked.

"Yep," Tom said laughing, "that could definitely be a body cue. Anything that signals a biological change when your emotions kick in. And since I believe God created us this way for good reason, I asked Brad, 'Why do you think God designed us to experience these internal body cues?' Brad answered my question with a question of his own: 'Have you heard of the fight-or-flight response?'"

A look of recognition came across some faces and heads nodded.

"By your response, I can see that you have heard of that concept, too. Well, I believe God built into each of us certain positive, purposeful reactions to stress. The fight-or-flight instincts are part of His design. He created us so that certain physical, noticeable changes occur without us having to think about them. Our bodies give us plenty of clues, but—"

Suddenly Tom's eyes widened as he looked toward the ceiling. "Duck!" he yelled.

Everyone reacted instinctively, and then when they saw there was no danger, they relaxed, laughing.

"Gotcha," Tom grinned. "You all just demonstrated one God-given reason for our fight-or-flight response. And from the looks of my little experiment, you didn't have to think very hard about what to do, did you?"

They all agreed.

"What happens," he continued, "when you're riding your bike or walking and you hear a car approaching closely behind you?"

"You move as far from his lane as you can," replied Mike.

"Exactly. So you see how God fitted us at the factory with standard equipment that helps us react quickly in times of stress.

"When our fight-or-flight instincts kick in, certain muscles tighten and the body immediately prepares itself for an appropriate reaction to danger. The trouble is, sometimes we get wound so tight, like the mainspring of a watch, that we can't really tell the difference between a relaxed state and a stressed state. And when that happens and our fight-or-flight reaction kicks in, we're already pegging the meter, and wham, it doesn't take much to put us over the edge emotionally. Am I making sense?"

They nodded.

Learning to Feel the Difference between "Relaxed" and "Stressed"

"The best way to learn what your body cues feel like is to learn the difference between feeling stressed and feeling relaxed. So we're going to practice a little bit with some fun and simple exercises to help us learn to pay attention to the differences between stress and relaxation."

"If you say so," Vicki said tentatively.

"I was a little apprehensive about some of this stuff when Tom and I went through it, Vick," Kaycee said. "But these exercises are great. I think you'll have fun with them."

Vicki smiled and shrugged as if to say, *I'm not so sure, but I'll give it a shot.*

Tom introduced the exercise. "Now if I were to lead you through this exercise so you'd get the most benefit, it would take from twenty to forty minutes, so I'll do a shorter version tonight. But once you learn the basics, you can do the whole routine at home, when you have time to really stretch out and concentrate on your entire body."

Sandi said, "If I stretch out right now, I won't *have* to concentrate. I'd be out like a light in thirty seconds!"

Tom laughed with the others. "I'll make sure not to put you completely to sleep. We'll just work on the upper body, especially the fingers, arms, and shoulders. Ready to give it a go?"

People nodded yes, took deep breaths, and prepared for instructions.

"Okay. First, when I say go, I'd like you to tighten your fingers into a fist, on both hands, and hold them as tight as you can for three seconds. Then I'll tell you to relax and exhale. As you do, I want you to be aware of the muscles you've just tensed and feel the difference between the tension and the new relaxed state. Try not to use any other muscles—just the fingers as a fist. Ready? Go."

Vicki scowled, squirmed in her chair, looked around at everyone else, and finally placed her hands in her lap and clenched her fingers into a fist.

Tom paused long enough to allow everybody to pay attention to their fists. Knuckles were white, and Sandi, who had her eyes closed, grimaced a bit from the tension.

"Okay," Tom said in a smooth voice, "now exhale, relax your fingers, and be aware of the difference between *tense* and *relaxed.*"

Sandi kept her eyes shut as she said, "Wake me up when we're ready for dessert."

Others chuckled but continued to concentrate.

After a few seconds, Tom said, "Now, let's pause for just a moment. Stay relaxed. Do your fingers and hands feel any different than they did just a minute ago?"

A couple of heads nodded.

"Good. The most important part of this exercise is learning to be aware of the differences, so pay close attention to how your muscles feel as you are relaxing. Now try to tense only your forearm muscles. We'll hold them tight for three seconds, exhale, relax, and be aware. Ready? Go."

The group followed Tom's commands as he led them through the same exercise with their forearms, upper arms, shoulders, and chest muscles. When they were through, Vicki, sounding surprised, said, "Wow. I don't think I've been this relaxed in weeks. It feels great." She took another long, deep breath, looking more peaceful than the group had ever seen her.

"It does, doesn't it?" Tom agreed.

■ Pause here, or if you aren't in a position to do so, plan a time when you can work through the following muscle groups just as Tom's group did. Tense each specific area for three seconds, then exhale and relax, paying

Build a Skill close attention to how your muscles feel.

MUSCLE GROUP 1:

   a. Forehead and eyes

   b. Cheeks

   c. Chin

   d. Shoulders up to your ears

MUSCLE GROUP 2:

   a. Fingers

   b. Forearms

   c. Upper arms

   d. Chest

MUSCLE GROUP 3:

   a. Stomach

   b. Upper legs

   c. Lower legs

   d. Feet, toes

Tom continued, "Brad told us that some people, if they are prone to being more tense than others, from the moment their eyes fly open in the morning are already at about a thirty or forty on the Emotion Thermometer. They just wake up and tense up, without even being aware that they are wound so tightly. Just becoming aware of how tense we are can help us monitor how we're doing so we can keep track of our progress throughout the day."

"Sometimes," said Sandi, "when I'm on call and I get jangled out of bed at 3 A.M. to rush to the hospital, I wake up and I'm tied in knots. And yet we're expected to be totally focused and ready for action when we get to the emergency room."

"Good example, Sandi. By the time we get through all this material, you'll have some great ammunition with which to fight back when those phone calls trigger extra tension.

"Now that you are finished tensing and relaxing, do any of the rest of you notice something observable about the differences in your muscles?"

"You know what?" Vicki offered, still looking like her arms were lead weights. "I think I do. I don't think I ever realized before now just how tight my chest usually is *most* of the time. When I *really* relaxed, my breathing slowed *way* down and I felt like muscles in my upper body finally loosened up. I'm breathing more deeply right now than I've been able to in a long time. It's great!"

People applauded. "You go, girl," said Sandi.

"That really is a breakthrough, Vicki," said Tom. "You're catching on. See how easy some of this stuff is? It's not rocket science. It's really only making you aware of how God put you together. As I said before, we are, as the Bible says, 'fearfully and wonderfully made,' and God provided us with all the equipment we need to recognize what's going on inside our bodies. We're just learning how to pay more attention to the bodies God gave us."

Kaycee added, "I thought that the relaxation exercises alone were worth taking the class. Now, when I'm feeling tension, I can actually make some time to focus on relaxing for a bit. Even just a couple of minutes can help keep me from knotting up during a busy day."

"That's true, Kayc," said Tom. "Just being aware that you *do* have some control over what your body is doing is a real big step in the right direction. Let's take a quick break, and then we'll work on a couple of *really* fun exercises to help these concepts come alive."

chapter six

LEAVE THE WATER BEFORE THE SHARK ATTACKS

Learning to Use the Emotion Thermometer

Now," Tom picked up where he had left off before the break, "I'd like to continue this body-cue exercise by asking you to pay close attention to what your body is telling you through its tension.

"The best way for me to do that in this group setting is to take you all on a little ride in your mind. Even though you'll all be reacting to the same scenario, each of your cues may be a little different. It'll be interesting to see what each of you feels as you do your freeze-frame moments to listen to what your body is telling you. For now, let's practice listening to body cues as you mentally react to a stressful situation. Ready to travel?"

Group members shifted in their seats and prepared for further instructions.

"Okay, close your eyes. You are now in your car, driving along a tree-lined country road in the fall. The trees are filled with colors—crimson, orange, red, yellow. Some postcard-perfect clouds make the sky seem even bluer than usual. Your windows are rolled down and you feel the breeze—a perfect 72 degrees. Now, listen to your body cues. Feel various parts of your body. Are you feeling good?"

Smiles told the story.

The Emotion Thermometer

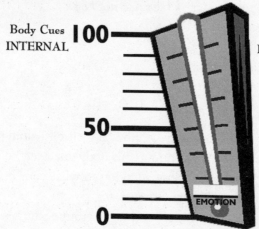

"Good. Freeze-frame this moment. Now open your eyes and note where you would put your feelings on the Emotion Thermometer. If you're really relaxed, then put your mark down around a zero. At each freeze-frame moment, I'll ask you to note how you are feeling, especially which parts of your body are reacting to stress and how intense the feeling is.

"Close your eyes again. As you drive along in this beautiful setting, miles away from the pressure of your jobs and family responsibilities, you glance down and see your gas gauge. The needle is dangerously close to empty, and the little yellow warning light is on."

People visibly changed position in their seats.

"Now freeze-frame. What are you feeling at this moment? What is your body doing? Check yourself for muscles that are tense in contrast to a moment ago. Feel any differences? If so, where? How intense is the feeling? Where are you on the emotion thermometer?"

Each member concentrated, paying attention to the bodily reaction to the stress induced by Tom's story. Some jotted down a word or two on the left side of their thermometer chart. Others just stared ahead, heads cocked to one side, as though listening for their feelings.

"I don't get it," said Vicki. "All I feel is mad."

"At what or whom?" Tom asked.

"At my husband for not filling up the gas tank on my car like he was supposed to!"

The group's concentration was broken for a moment by laughter, but Tom brought them back to focus.

"Close your eyes again. You drive along this country road for five more miles with no sight of civilization. Freeze your mind's video here and inspect your body for more cues."

They did so, and several members appeared visibly more agitated than a moment earlier.

"What parts of your body are tense? How intense is the change? Where are you on the thermometer? Make a mark."

He paused as people thought and wrote.

"Now you look up and see a sign. It's the entrance ramp to a major freeway. Now what do you feel?"

More smiles. More notes were written.

"You drive along the freeway, looking for a gas station, glancing down at the needle of your gas gauge. It's dropping even further below the *Empty* level. You are wondering just how many miles you can go on empty after the light has come on. You check your odometer and realize that you've now traveled twenty miles. How does your body feel at this moment? Evaluate your intensity level."

More introspection. Most of the group were now so caught up in the imaginary road trip that they had stopped taking notes.

"Suddenly you see a sign at the side of the freeway. It says, *Gas, Food, 1 Mile*. Now what is your body telling you? How far down the thermometer did you come?"

Several took deep breaths and their shoulders relaxed slightly.

"You take the exit, turn right, and find yourself on a narrow two-lane road that quickly becomes a dirt road. There is no gas station in sight. You feel the car's engine sputter slightly. What is your body telling you? Rate your intensity."

A look of near-panic swept across Sandi's face as her breathing became shallow and more rapid.

"Ah," Tom continued, with a soothing tone and the sound of relief in his voice. "*There* it is. A gas station, up ahead only about a quarter of a mile, on the right. Freeze-frame. What's your body telling you now? Where's your intensity level?"

Sandi wiped her hand across her forehead and said aloud, "Whew!"

"You clear a grove of trees that has nearly hidden the gas station, and it's obvious you are going to make it to the pump before the car quits. But now you see about sixteen *big* motorcycles, and even *bigger* motorcycle owners, all in tattered blue jeans and most not wearing shirts—plenty of tattoos—and some wearing black leather vests over their hairy chests. Almost all of them have beards and long hair. Freeze-frame again. Now what is your body telling you about what you are feeling? How high up on the thermometer did you go?"

"If I get out of this one alive, I'm gonna kill my husband."

People kept their eyes shut but smiled at Vicki's comment. Most continued to concentrate, awaiting Tom's next suggestion.

"You pull up to the gas pump, get out, smile, and nod at a couple of the burly bikers. They just mill around, staring at you, as you fill your car's tank. Now it appears you have to walk right through the middle of the group to pay for the gas. Freeze-frame. How does your body feel now? Check each area: legs, abdomen, chest, arms, shoulders. Mark your level of intensity."

Facial expressions varied and some actually nodded, as though addressing the imaginary bikers on their way to the clerk.

"The bikers step back and form an aisle, allowing you to walk to the counter, where you pay for the gas. You walk back to your car, get inside, pull back onto the dirt road, heading for the freeway. Just out of sight from the gas station, you hit the electric door lock button. Freeze-frame again. What is your body doing? How intense?"

"Thank you, Jesus!" Sandi said.

"You hop back on the freeway, heading back toward home, and check your gas gauge again. Full. And you roll down your windows again to enjoy the fall breeze and the incredible colors. You happen to glance in your rearview mirror and there they are, the huge pack of bikers, roaring up fast behind you. Freeze again. What is your body doing? Don't forget to evaluate the level of intensity."

Sandi spoke again, "Tom, you are a sneaky one. Just when I

thought you'd gotten me out of that gas station..."

Tom stayed with the story. "The bikers pull into the left lane and pass you, each one smiling and waving a friendly hello as they do. Freeze-frame again. What are your body's cues telling you? Where are you on the thermometer?"

"That's another fine mess you've gotten me out of," Sandi said, relief in her voice.

They all laughed.

"Okay, open your eyes. Now let's take a minute to jot down the various observations you made about your internal body cues, making sure you noted how intense the reactions were at each freeze-frame moment along the way."

Vicki spoke first. "I was frustrated. Much of the time I was just feeling angry. I had a hard time feeling anything else. Just *mad.*"

"Well, you're not alone, Vicki. Not many of us have been taught to be this aware of what's going on inside us when we experience emotions. In fact, we are such creatures of habit that often we'll go through all sorts of steps—from trigger to action—without even thinking about what has happened to get us there. Don't feel bad if you don't recognize these things right away."

Different Cues for Different People

"Y'all want to know somethin' weird?" Sandi said. "Just now, when you were explaining that stuff to Vicki, I noticed something that might be one of my body cues."

"What's that?"

"I've had this little eye twitch thing goin' on for months now, just off and on. And when I started feeling stressed, the corner of my left eye would twitch. Just a little bit. People at work tell me they can't see it, but it sure feels strange to me. I'll bet that's one of my cues. Could it be?"

"It's very possible," Tom replied. "Of course, each person has different cues because we all have different backgrounds and we're all put together differently, but that could certainly be one of the subtle cues your body gives you, Sandi. Maybe as we learn to chart our emotional cues over several days, it will pop up as something that happens often. If that's the case, and if it's related to a certain type of trigger, then you will have found yourself an indicator—something to warn you of stress that could build up inside and create big problems."

"Now, there," Sandi said, "it's just stopped. Just talking about it made it go away. Isn't that weird?"

"Well, once again you've just demonstrated something important to the rest of us. Brad told us that often, once we've recognized a particular emotion, just simply talking about it may actually help diminish its intensity. Isn't that cool? Wouldn't it be great if we could do that physically? If we could just take our temperature when we're running a fever, and the very act of taking our temperature would help bring it down? With our emotions, that's kind of what happens. Just becoming aware of what's going on inside us helps us think through our response to it. But that's really only scratching the surface. There's still so much good stuff to explore. I can't wait for you guys to make some of the discoveries I made with this material."

External Cues Are Observable Behaviors

Vicki sighed and crossed her arms. "I can't even figure out what my body is doing when I'm angry. How can I get to the 'good stuff' when I can't even seem to get this far?"

"You've just done something wonderful," said Tom.

She looked startled. "I have?"

"Yes. Look at your arms."

She looked down and saw that they were crossed. She uncrossed them, self-consciously. "Yeah? So?"

"You've just demonstrated a behavior, an outwardly recognizable signal. Something that other people notice about us when we are experiencing an emotion."

"So I'm demonstrating my emotions to others without even recognizing them myself?"

"Exactly. But Vicki, that's not a *bad* thing. We all do that. Much of the time, in fact. That's why becoming more aware of what's going on *inside* is so important. There's a good chance we'll learn to recognize these cues even before they are noticed by others. That gives us a chance to allow the Holy Spirit to intervene *before* we allow our emotions to build up and cause us to do something we'll regret later."

"May I offer just one possible analogy?" Ron asked politely.

"Absolutely."

"It seemed to click with me that my internal responses to emotion were sort of like those musical cues in movies, like the cello music they play just before the shark comes out in *Jaws*. They are like a foreshadowing of what's about to happen."

Tom said, "That's a good way to think of these internal cues. Consider them God's cello music, letting you know that the emotion is under the surface and approaching quickly. Now, let's see if we can help Vicki for a second by telling what cues you each recognized about yourselves. Maybe some of these will apply to you, too, Vicki."

She rolled her eyes. "Okay. I'll try."

Sandi started. "When I first looked at my gas gauge, I noticed that the muscles in my neck kind of tensed up. That's probably where I get those headaches. I get 'em when I've been really stressed and when I'm sitting all hunched up at the computer at the nurse's station."

"I felt my stomach tighten a little," said Mike. "Maybe that's why I can't eat when I'm nervous or angry."

"Oh honey," Sandi said. "I wish I had *your* body cues. When I get stressed, eatin's about all I *wanna* do!"

Tom continued his attempt to help. "Vicki, thinking back to our exercise, did you notice any of those kinds of things going on inside yourself?"

She shook her head, obviously frustrated with herself.

"That's okay. This is a learning process, and it can take time. Maybe after you've charted your feelings for a week or so, you'll begin to recognize some patterns about how your body reacts. It's perfectly normal not to recognize the cues right away. Stay with it, okay?

"Now, let's look at the right side of the chart, the *External* side. Can some of you name some external behaviors people might exhibit when they get to different levels of anger?"

"I know one," said Vicki. "Crossed arms."

Laughter.

"How about drumming fingers?" Mike asked. "I know someone who starts drumming his fingers on the table, or on his knee, whenever he starts to get agitated, just before he gets angry."

Everyone looked at each other, and at their own hands, each hoping he or she wasn't the culprit. "No, I didn't mean you guys. It's *me*. I just discovered it. Someone at work told me to quit drumming the other day, and I wasn't even aware I was doing it.

I think that's one of my outward behaviors."

Tom gave a thumbs-up sign. "Good observation, Mike. You'll probably notice that the higher up we go on our thermometers, the more obvious the behaviors. We could probably go on up the thermometer and add some more examples, like pacing, or shouting, or smashing a plate on the floor, or hitting something...."

"Or some*one*," Vicki blurted, then acted surprised that those words had come out of her mouth. She added, "Well, I *was* all set to whack my husband when I got home!"

"And we've all felt that way at one time or another," Tom agreed. "The cool part of these exercises is that we will be getting to know our internal and external body cues so that we get *tipped* off before we get *ticked* off."

Then, in his exaggerated teacher voice, Tom said, "My body cues are my friends. Can you say that with me, class?"

"My body cues are my friends," they all mimicked, then cracked up.

Tom said, "If you'll work hard on these exercises, you'll become good friends with your internal cues. And if you'll learn to trust your good friends, they will warn you that you are raising the temperature of your emotion thermometer and headed for trouble."

"You can learn to hear the cello music before the shark attacks," added Ron. "Then you can get out of the water before you get bit."

"Exactly, Ron. Now, can someone tell me why these seemingly negative emotions can be considered gifts from God?"

"Say what?" asked Sandi.

"Think about it," Tom continued. "Feelings such as anger, sadness, anxiety, and fear can actually be *good* things if we understand their God-designed purposes."

"Hmm, that's interesting, since I normally think of those feelings as curses rather than as blessings," Ron said. "But I suppose there *are* some helpful aspects to them. Like pain, for instance. Without it, we aren't warned that we could get hurt. I've read that people with diseases like leprosy, which kills off nerve endings, have to be careful because they can hurt themselves and not even know it."

"Yeah," Mike said. "And anger and aggression can give us the strength to protect ourselves or save a damsel in distress or something. Like those fight-or-flight instincts you mentioned."

"Good examples, guys. Since God made us, including all the emotions that came installed at the factory, those emotions must be there for a good reason. The problem lies with *our response* to the feelings. When we get to the Flesh/Spirit stage next week, we'll zero in on how we can cooperate with the Holy Spirit, allowing Him to direct us through the impulse process so the outcome is what *He* intended."

Build a Skill

■ Use the following Emotion Thermometer activity to help raise your awareness of the body cues and behaviors that accompany your core emotions. You may find it most helpful to build a separate thermometer (using a separate sheet) for each of the following emotions:

Happy

Sad

Anxious

Calm

1. Think of a time when you were really (fill in the emotion you are working on) _____.

2. What picture comes to mind as you think of that emotion?_____.

3. Now insert that picture into a motion-picture clip and run it in your mind, much as Tom's group did with his story about running low on gas. As you relive the event that caused your specified emotion, what do you observe about your body cues? _____. Rate the intensity of emotion you are experiencing on your Emotion Thermometer.

4. What *internal changes* in your body do you notice at this moment? _____.

5. What *external behaviors* do you observe, either about yourself or about others, related to that specific emotion? _____.
Rate the intensity of your external behaviors on the thermometer.

■ Note: If you are having trouble identifying internal body cues related to each of these emotions, it might help to listen to others in a group as they discuss their cues. Then you may begin to notice similar cues in your own body's response to certain emotions. Don't feel badly if you don't recognize the cues right away. As it did for Vicki, sometimes it takes practice to become aware of what your body is doing in response to a specific emotion. Just being aware of the process will eventually help you become more aware of your responses to feelings.

chapter seven

WHERE THERE'S A WILL

The Flesh vs. the Spirit, Part 1

O kay gang, this is where we get to the good stuff!" Tom announced, calling the group to a semblance of order.

"Finally, we get to the *heart* of the impulse process. So far, we've learned how thoughts are formed, starting with a trigger of some sort. That trigger brings to mind a thought, in the form of a picture or a sound bite. Those thoughts are imprinted with emotions. When you insert them into a motion-picture or audio clip and run them over and over, your feelings raise the heat of your emotional thermometer until it reaches the flash point. Then you take action, motivated by those feelings. Is everyone with me up to this point?

They all nodded.

"Great! Well, group, I've got great news for you. I get to step back and let the real pro take over for an evening…"

"You mean Ron's going to lead?" Vicki asked.

"Well, as much as I trust he would do a good job, no. Ron will have his chance when we can start another group like this one. But for now, I'd like to officially introduce you to someone most of you met as we came in tonight. Brad Rogers is the guy who taught this stuff to Kaycee and me, and the man I keep referring to. This is *the* man himself, a professional counselor, a man who compiled all this material, and a man who has used his God-given skills to help hundreds of others manage their emotions and impulses in ways that honor the Lord. Brad, welcome."

The group applauded.

"Well," Brad began, "I can certainly see what Tom meant when he told me you were an enthusiastic group."

They gave him another brief ovation.

"Well," said Brad, "maybe you should wait until *after* tonight's class before you decide how much cheering you should do. But thank you for the warm welcome. I've been looking forward to meeting you ever since Tom started bragging about you several weeks ago. Tom and Kaycee soaked up this material when I taught the class they took, and I knew they'd do a great job passing it along to others. I'm grateful, Tom, that you and Kaycee have allowed me to present this phase of the process, since it gives me a chance to teach what I believe is the most important part.

"Tonight, we're going to look at the one phase of the impulse process in which we can turn what could become negative impulses into positive thoughts, leading to positive feelings, motivating us to positive actions. Those actions then lead to wonderful consequences—lasting rewards instead of painful punishment; the sweet fruit of the Holy Spirit instead of the rotten fruit of the flesh."

Tom enjoyed watching the class respond to Brad's gentle authority. They were less boisterous and more attentive.

"First," Brad said, passing around some papers, "let's look at what the heart is. Take a peek at this handout titled *Your Heart Is....* Did you ever stop to think just how important your heart is to you? Glance down through the list and notice all the important things that take place in your heart."

Your Heart Is...

1. THE CENTER OF YOUR PURPOSEFUL THOUGHT:

Your heart "knows." (Proverbs 14:10)
Your heart "understands." (Acts 16:14)
You can "stand steadfast" in your heart. (1 Corinthians 7:37)

2. THE SEAT OF YOUR EMOTIONS:

You can have a "joyful heart." (Isaiah 65:14)
You can have a "heavy heart." (Proverbs 25:20)
You can have an "anxious heart." (Proverbs 12:25)

3. THE SEAT OF YOUR WILL:

You can desire to do God's will. (Psalm 40:8)
You can hide things in your heart and then act on them later. (Luke 2:19)
You can store in your heart either good or evil treasure. (Luke 6:45)
You can presume in your heart to do something. (Esther 7:5)

4. THE SEAT OF YOUR CONSCIENCE:

You can know you belong to the truth, because your heart (conscience) convicts (condemns) you when you stray from the truth. (1 John 3:19)

5. THE RESIDENCE OF GOD'S HOLY SPIRIT:

Your heart can be the field for the seed of His divine word. (Matthew 13:19)
Your heart can be the dwelling place of Christ in you. (Ephesians 3:17)
Your heart can be the resting place for God's peace. (Colossians 3:15)
Your heart can be the container of God's love. (Romans 5:5)
Your heart can be the place of communion with God. (Ephesians 5:19)
Your heart can be the door where God enters your life. (Romans 10:9–10; Revelation 3:20)

The group took a few moments to skim the handout. "Whew," Sandi said, "as a nurse I knew the heart was important to our physical beings, but I never dreamed the heart was that important to the spiritual part of us."

"Yes, indeed," Brad said. "God certainly intended that our hearts become vital parts of our being. Now, I want to show you a relationship that is vital to the whole impulse development process. It's a relationship between your heart and your mind. Look at this next sheet titled *In Your Mind*...."

In Your Mind...

1. CONVICTIONS ARE FORMED:

You can do something in all earnestness of mind. (Deuteronomy 18:6)

2. LOYALTIES ARE FORMED:

You can serve someone with a whole heart and a willing mind. (1 Chronicles 28:9)

3. THE DECISION TO LOVE IS MADE:

You can love someone with all your heart and with all your soul and with all your strength and with all your mind. (Luke 10:27)

4. RENEWAL TAKES PLACE:

You can be renewed in the spirit of your mind. (Ephesians 4:23)

5. LAWS ARE KEPT:

You can allow someone to put their laws in your minds and write them on your hearts. (Hebrews 8:10)

Brad paused for a moment to allow members to look over the handout. Then he asked, "See the very first item on the list? You can do something in all earnestness of mind. That sounds a lot like doing something 'with all your heart,' doesn't it?"

People nodded their heads.

He then asked, "And look at numbers two, three, and five. Do you see anything common to each of those three items?"

Ron spoke up quickly. "Each of them contains sentences with both the words *heart* and *mind* in them."

"Precisely," said Brad. "The Old Testament concept of the heart was so tied together with what we think of as the word mind, that you could almost substitute mind for heart in many instances—and you'd be on target. Let me take it one step further. If I were to 'know in my heart' that it was wrong to do something, what would I mean by that?"

Mike said, "That your conscience told you it was wrong?"

"Good. So let me ask you, where's your conscience located? In that blood-pumping muscle in your chest?"

People chuckled as they caught Brad's drift.

"You see, we are so used to saying 'heart' when we could easily say 'mind' that we forget how important our mind is in this impulse-development process. It's very important that we see the connection because it will make a huge difference in whether we're successful at deflecting Satan's darts."

"So you're saying that our hearts and minds are basically the same thing, right?" Vicki asked.

Brad nodded.

"Then could we write the word *mind* next to the heart on our Impulse Process Chart?"

"That's a great idea. If it helps you maintain the biblical concept of heart and mind, do it. Let me also add one more important ingredient to the heart/mind concept. See number two, where it says *Loyalties are formed?*"

They did.

"The verse used to illustrate this idea comes from 1 Chronicles, where King David is giving instructions to his son, Solomon. He urges his son to serve God with 'wholehearted devotion,' and with 'a willing mind.' One translation says *a whole heart* instead of *wholehearted*. But you get the picture, right? What I'd like you to notice is the word *willing* in that sentence. From this Bible verse, where would you think the will is formed?"

"In the mind," Mike answered.

"Good."

Ron added, "And yet when you look back at the verses related to the heart, it shows that the heart is the seat of the will. So, it would appear that our will is developed in both our hearts and our minds."

"Good again," Brad said. He turned to Tom. "I see what you mean about these people. Sharp!"

They all smiled.

"You're getting the key point here," Brad said. "You see, our culture has led us to believe that when we 'feel' something in our hearts, we have to separate those feelings from our minds and will. But the biblical view of the heart and mind is that they are *both* involved in developing our wills."

Will Formed in Both Heart and Mind

Brad started another stack of papers around the room. "You'll see in this next handout that I've actually used the terms *heart* and *mind* together. I've put a slash between them, but I want you to start thinking of the heart and mind together, okay? Now the Bible shows us that there is a serious conflict going on inside these hearts-slash-minds of ours.

"Paul the apostle uses some imagery from his knowledge of wars and battles in his day. Take a look at the difference between what's on the left side and what's on the right side."

IN YOUR HEART/MIND, THERE'S A WAR GOING ON. IN YOUR HEART/MIND, YOU HAVE...

THE FLESH	AT WAR WITH	THE SPIRIT
(combustible material)		(nonflammable material)
A prideful heart/mind. (1 John 2:16)		A humble heart/mind. (1 John 2:14)
A hardened heart/mind. (Isaiah 6:10)		A softened heart/mind. (Luke 8:15)
A sinful heart/mind. (Galatians 5:19–21)		A Spirit-controlled heart/mind. (Galatians 5:22–24)

"Do you notice the types of combustible material under *The Flesh?*" Brad asked, waiting for the group to scan the sheet and respond.

"Well, it appears that these are all things related to our natural tendencies, our sinful nature."

"Exactly right," answered Brad. "And you must be Ron."

"Yes," Ron replied. "Has Tom been telling you stories about us?"

"He has—mostly good," Brad said, grinning. "And I thought the meticulous notes you're taking in that five-inch-thick notebook was a good hint."

The group laughed.

Brad kept the pace going. "Now, as the flesh, or sinful nature, wars with the spirit, the heart becomes a battleground between evil and good. Chances are we've *all* experienced the frustration and trauma of those battles—many of which take place deep inside where the only person who knows about them is us. Am I right, or way off base?"

Everyone nodded in the affirmative.

"Well, the apostle Paul was a man who learned a lot about this battle between our tendency to sin and our desire to draw close to God. He penned some helpful words in his letter to the church in Rome. Look at the next sheet I'm handing around. I've grabbed some excerpts from Paul's passage in Romans to highlight this internal war between the flesh and the Spirit. Whoever wants to volunteer, read the first sentence on the left side. Then someone else read the one opposite, on the right. And so on, so we can crisscross our way down the page. Listen to Paul's inner struggle as you read."

THE FLESH	VS.	THE SPIRIT
	(Romans 7:15–8:2)	
"For what I want to do, I do not do."		"For I have the desire to do what is good…"
"…but I cannot carry it out."		"When I want to do good…"
"…evil is right there with me."		"For in my inner being, I delight in God's law…"
"…but I see another law at work… waging war against the law of my mind, and making me a prisoner of sin at work within my members."		
"Who will rescue me from this body of death?"		"Thanks be to God—through Jesus Christ our Lord!"
		"Therefore, there is now no condemnation for those who are in Christ Jesus, because through Christ Jesus the law of the Spirit of life set me free from the law of sin and death."

"Now *that's* a conflict if ever I read about one," Brad said as the group finished reading the verses aloud. "And as good as we may appear to other people around us, all of us have experienced the same struggles as Paul with that pesky old nature—that 'flesh' as he calls it. I know I sure have. But from the last verse, we can see that Paul found a strategy to win the war that takes place in our heart/minds. This strategy is a *person*. Jesus Christ."

Sandi clapped her hands together. "Amen! Preach it, Brother Brad!"

Most of the group chuckled and nodded. Vicki rolled her eyes.

Brad smiled at Sandi's encouragement. "The first thing we have to have in place for any of these concepts to work is Jesus Christ. People who have been believers in Christ for a long time may assume this—but I don't want to miss this important step. The very first step—and the most important—anybody can take in this whole process is to invite Jesus into their hearts and minds. All it takes is a heartfelt, simple prayer, something like, 'Jesus, I realize I need You as my personal Lord and Savior. Please send Your Holy Spirit to live in my heart and mind. I want a personal relationship with You. I turn my life over to You. Thank You for coming into my heart. Amen.'"

He continued, "How many of you, at some point in your lives, have said a prayer something like this?" Everyone in the room raised a hand.

"Excellent. I thought so. But I always want to be sure that everyone understands this important prerequisite. If one hasn't received Jesus Christ as Savior and Lord, the Holy Spirit won't be residing within him. And without His Spirit in us it is virtually impossible to win the battle between the flesh and the Spirit."

Vicki spoke up. "Brad, can I ask you something?"

"Of course."

"Well, I know about Jesus being God's Son. I truly believe He died on the cross to pay the penalty for my sin. I *know* that. I've accepted His gift of grace in my life. And I've heard all the sermons about 'letting go and letting God.' But my question is, *how?* How do you get a grip on these impulses?"

The Imp

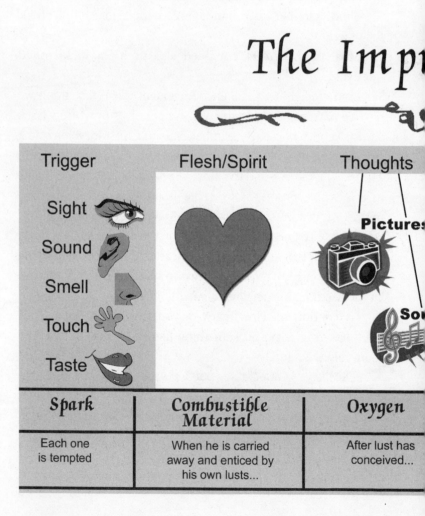

Spark	Combustible Material	Oxygen
Each one is tempted	When he is carried away and enticed by his own lusts...	After lust has conceived...

Brad nodded to acknowledge Vicki's good question. "In fact, that was *my* question back when I first started doing counseling for a living. I felt like some of the tools I was working with were inadequate to get to the real root of people's impulse-control problems. That's when I started applying what I learned from the Bible to the counseling tools that did seem be working.

se Process

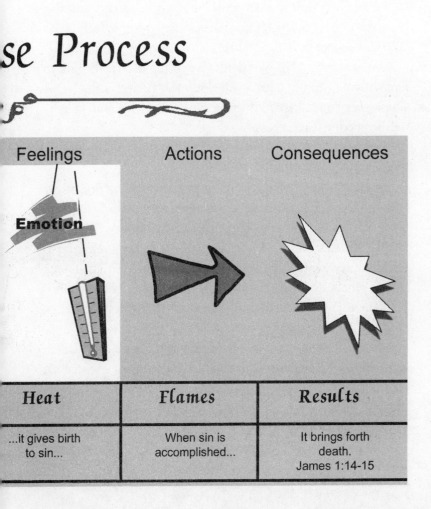

Feelings	Actions	Consequences
Emotion		

Heat	Flames	Results
...it gives birth to sin...	When sin is accomplished...	It brings forth death. James 1:14-15

"The reason these counseling techniques work so well is that they are based on the way God put us together. Since God created us for the purpose of knowing Him, this material helps us cooperate with Him in His purpose. What you're learning through this material is how God put you together and how to let Him work in you to gain victory over the flesh. He created you with an inner desire to know Him. He is available, through His Holy Spirit, to reside in your heart/mind. Once you get to know Him, on a personal level, some of these fairly simple techniques help you cooperate with what He's already doing in your life.

"As you pour His Word into your minds, He begins to replace your sinful, selfish will with His perfect will. It's so simple, yet I'm still amazed to see how people become literally transformed in the process."

Sandi was grinning ear to ear. "That's right. Preach it. Amen, brother."

Brad chuckled. "Sandi, I wish you were in every one of my classes. That kind of response gets me fired up and ready to teach.

"Let's take a look at a chart that should be very familiar to you by now. It's almost identical to one you've been referring to these first few weeks, but with one added element. Can anyone tell me what's new?" He handed out the *Impulse Process* chart.

"There's a verse from James spread across the bottom," Mike observed.

"Right. This verse, written by the half brother of Christ, really shows where this whole impulse process goes if we are *not* controlled by the Holy Spirit. You have already studied about triggers, right?"

They nodded.

"Well, let's work our way across the chart, following this

verse from left to right, and see how it matches up with what you've learned so far."

Satan's Weapons

"What happens, way back at the trigger stage, is that Satan shoots his weapons at us. Paul calls them "fiery darts." He uses that term in the passage in Ephesians 6 where he talks about putting on the armor of God. You're probably all pretty familiar with that passage. If not, jot down *Ephesians 6* on your chart and read up on the armor when you get home tonight. It has a lot of great implications for the process we're learning about."

A couple of members jotted the reference in their notes.

"To give you a little background about this unusual weapon, Paul knew that it was common in those days for soldiers to dip the tips of short, wooden missiles into a flammable substance like pitch. Pitch is kind of like tree sap. Have you ever seen how quickly pine sap goes up in flames? If you've ever gone camping, or if you have a fireplace, you've probably found that a small piece of dry pine with lots of sap running through it lights up pretty quickly.

"That pine makes a great fire starter because once it's ignited, highly combustible sap bursts into flame, and the sticky, gooey burning substance ignites all flammable surfaces around it. It was a similar molten mess that made the darts such useful weapons back in Paul's day."

Brad continued, "This stuff was really a fiery mess. And unlike longer arrows, shot over longer distances by archers, these shorter 'darts' were shot into the enemy camp at closer range. That means the enemy had to creep close enough to scope out vulnerable targets. These stealthy attackers knew the purpose of their weapons. They weren't trying to mortally wound people by putting holes in them. They were trying to hit targets that could be ignited by the burning pitch."

Ron was taking copious notes. The others listened attentively.

"Let me ask you something. If you had been a soldier back then and if you could have strategically aimed a dart at a combustible material, what kind of material would you have tried to hit?"

"Perhaps a tent made of cloth?" Ron ventured.

Mike added, "Or maybe a wooden shield?"

"Exactly. If you could fire your dart at those objects, it would damage or destroy the soldier's protection, leaving him exposed to further harm. In many cases, because of the lack of government funding for adequate military equipment—things haven't changed much in two thousand years, have they?—the soldier's shield wasn't covered by copper, tin, or brass. It was only bare, dry wood, often covered by leather, both of which were highly combustible. What do you think might happen if a flaming dart hit that kind of shield?"

Mike was obviously into this discussion. "The molten goo would splatter all over the shield's surface and the whole thing would become a flaming mess."

"Right again. The trick in using a fiery dart was threefold: first, a sneak attack; second, careful aim at a combustible target; and third, careful timing in its release. When used properly, these small but dangerous weapons, by spreading their burning payload, would do *far* more damage than an untreated arrow."

He looked at his watch.

"I've promised you a break, and this would be a great time to take one. When we come back, we'll look at the three destructive things Satan tries to do with his flaming missiles."

Build a Skill

■ Answering the following questions will help you remember what you've just learned about Satan's weapons.

1. What two-word picture does Paul use to describe Satan's weapons?

2. If the purpose of these weapons is not to kill, then why are they used?

3. Are these long-range or short-range weapons? Why?

chapter eight

SATAN'S BIG WHISPERING CAMPAIGN

The Flesh vs. the Spirit, Part 2

om whistled for the group's attention and turned the session back over to Brad.

"Thanks, Tom," Brad said. "We're talking tonight about
the flesh versus the Spirit. It's a big, ongoing battle, but if
we know and appropriate God's truth we're guaranteed to win."

"Then why don't we win more often?" Vicki asked. "Why do
we give in to our negative impulses so much?"

"Good, honest question, Vicki. Even though God is still much
smarter than Satan, the crafty old devil is no dummy. He sneaks
around, prowling like a stealthy soldier, looking for your areas of
vulnerability. He'll sneak up behind you, draw his bow and hold
it, take careful aim, and wait for just the right moment to release
his flaming missiles. Those missiles are the triggers for what he

wants to become negative thoughts, feelings, and actions."

"He really is sneaky, too," Sandi agreed. "He knows just when I'm the most tired and the most hungry. That's when he hits me with those dumb darts of his."

Brad picked up on Sandi's thought. "Isn't that the truth? Sounds a lot like Matthew chapter 4, where Satan tempted Jesus when Jesus was really tired and hungry. He knows when to attack us. And for most of us it's all those little annoying triggers, building one on top of another, that finally get to us. Have you ever gotten up on the wrong side of the bed, and all day it seemed like everything that could go wrong did?"

Vicki said, "Yeah, like yesterday. The first thing that happened was that I stubbed my toe on my dresser. Then I spilled coffee grounds all over the refrigerator and kitchen floor. Then I tripped over my son's backpack which he left on the floor by the back door. I thought, *Well, I'm going to have a lousy day.*"

Brad asked, "How did you deal with all those little darts?"

"Well," Vicki said, "I normally would have gotten really angry. But each time those little things happened, I started thinking about the Impulse Process chart. I mean, I could actually see the chart in my head. And I thought, *Aha, these are darts. They are triggers.*"

"And what went through your mind the moment you recognized the triggers?"

"Well, it's kind of funny, but I remember seeing the face of my son, who walked in right after I had tripped over his backpack. He looked at me like he was expecting me to explode at him. But instead, I stopped for a split second, thought about a dart bouncing off my shield of faith, and thought, *I'm not going to let these stupid darts ruin my day.* So I said, 'Son, please pick up your backpack and put it where it belongs.'"

"I'll bet he didn't know what to do with *that* response," Sandi said.

Vicki laughed. "No, he didn't. He looked at me like, *Who are you and what have you done with my mom?* I took a couple of deep breaths, cleaned up the coffee grounds, and finished getting ready for the day."

The group erupted in applause at Vicki's story.

"Vicki, that's *great,*" Brad said. "Even if you couldn't remember all the steps in this process we've been studying, you've been able to do the most important thing. When you were hit with Satan's darts, you realized that you had a choice. And you responded in the Spirit. Good for you."

Negative Thoughts Are Like Glowing Embers

"Let me take you just one simple step further. As you've demonstrated, Vicki, our enemy is good at sneaking up on us and firing away with his darts. How we respond to them makes a difference in how we will be affected. If we choose to allow the triggers to ignite negative thoughts, then we've started a downward spiral leading to negative actions. Those little negative thoughts begin to glow like tiny embers. Those negative thoughts are to the impulse process what oxygen is to an ember. You can almost picture someone cupping their hands, blowing air across the glowing embers. The more you blow, the more they glow. And so the more you replay the negative thoughts ignited by Satan's triggers, the hotter your emotions get. See how this all relates to the *Impulse Process* chart?"

They all checked their charts and responded affirmatively.

"That's why it's important to take captive those negative thoughts *immediately,* before they have a chance to blow across the embers in our hearts and minds. Let me ask a question. If we keep whipping up a whirlwind of negative thoughts, building negative feelings, what happens to the temperature of our Emotion Thermometer?"

Spiral of Negative Emotions

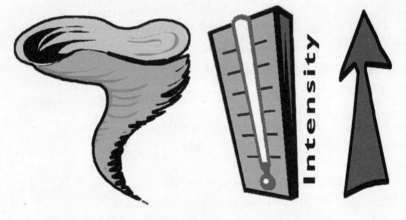

Sandi pointed skyward, indicating a rising thermometer.

"Right, Sandi. And when the temperature gets to the flash point, what's going to happen?"

"Whoosh," said Mike. "The fiery dart becomes a fiery furnace."

"Exactly. The negative feelings finally burst into flame and we act 'in the flesh,' rather than 'in the Spirit.' And of course, if the entire impulse process has led us down a negative spiral, what should we expect the consequences of our actions to be?"

They all said, "Negative."

"You betcha. Downright destructive. Our enemy is really good at taking God's positive impulses—those we act upon when we are walking in the Spirit—and perverting them, driving us to extremes, and turning what could have become positive impulses into destructive actions. That's what James was saying in the verse across the bottom of the *Impulse Process* chart.

"Look at the verse from James. Do you see the second column from the left, the one that says *Flesh/Spirit* at the top?"

They nodded.

"From the Scripture portion of the James passage at the bottom of that column, who is responsible for what happens *after* the dart hits your heart?"

"The one who has been hit."

"Right, Ron. According to this verse, Satan is only responsible for the temptation stage of the process. All he does is fire a dart and create a temptation. From that point on, the one who has been attacked has the ability to choose how to respond to that attack. And what makes the biggest difference in the whole process is what's in your heart at the time of the attack."

Building a Nonflammable Shield

"Let me describe for you what I believe makes for a strong shield—the kind that won't be burned by Satan's darts. In that Ephesians 6 passage we mentioned earlier, Paul tells us we should take up the 'shield of faith.' Faith in what or whom?"

"In God."

"And how do we know this God we're suppose to place our faith in? How do we know what God is like?"

Vicki said, "When we know His Son, we know what the Father is like too."

"You bet. Jesus actually said that about Himself in John 14:9: 'Anyone who has seen me has seen the Father.' However, Jesus was alive on earth only about thirty-three years. So since He's not

The Impr

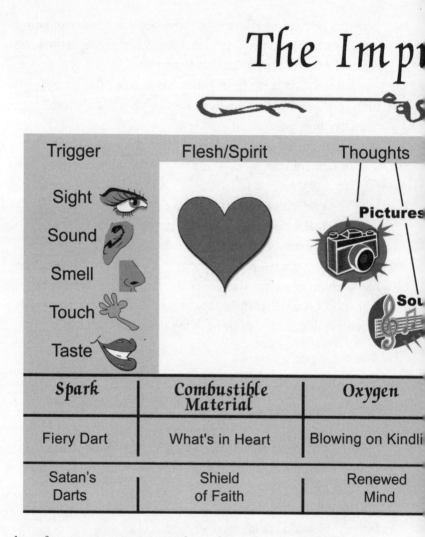

Trigger	Flesh/Spirit	Thoughts
Sight		Pictures
Sound		Sou
Smell		
Touch		
Taste		

Spark	Combustible Material	Oxygen
Fiery Dart	What's in Heart	Blowing on Kindli
Satan's Darts	Shield of Faith	Renewed Mind

here for us to see in person, how do we know about this God we're supposed to put our faith in?"

Tom held up his Bible.

"There you go," Brad said. "God really wanted to reveal Himself to us. He sent His Son to show us what He's like. And

se Process

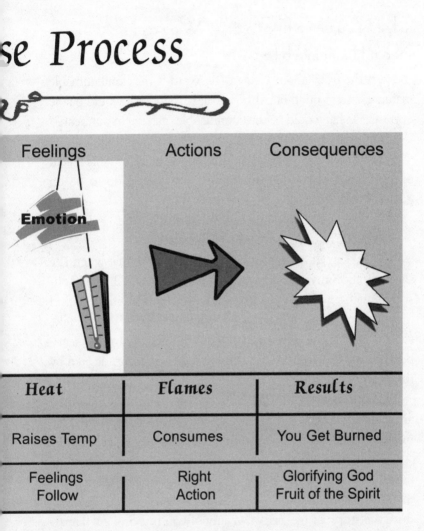

Feelings	Actions	Consequences
Heat	Flames	Results
Raises Temp	Consumes	You Get Burned
Feelings Follow	Right Action	Glorifying God Fruit of the Spirit

then He left a record of Himself for us, so we could know Him, even though it has been years since Christ walked the earth. He left us with what we now call the Bible. It's God's divinely inspired love letter, showing us all about Himself so we can personally know this God in whom we can place our faith."

The Truth of God's Word Is Nonflammable

"Now, if the truth about God in His Word is the nonflammable material used to build our shield of faith, then what would be the opposite? What would be the combustible material in our heart?"

"Anything that's *not* the truth about God," Ron said.

"Yes. And since we know how to build an unburnable shield of faith, then what does that suggest we should do to be on guard constantly?"

"Putting God's Word into our minds and hearts," said Sandi.

"Into our minds *slash* hearts," Mike clarified.

"And I can tell you from personal experience that when I've slacked off on my shield building—when I've failed to be consistent with my Bible reading and prayer time—then I find myself much more vulnerable to Satan's attacks. It doesn't take too many of those nasty darts to fire the embers in my heart, because I've allowed the stuff that's in there to go unprotected by the truth of God's Word."

Kaycee spoke. "Brad, do you have time to tell us the German army story, like you did when Tom and I took your class? That made so much sense in explaining Satan's strategy."

"Actually, that would be a good illustration to show how the lies of Satan creep into our hearts, creating a highly flammable material just waiting for spontaneous combustion. But to introduce the story, let me ask: Have any of you heard of a whispering campaign? Do you know what that is?"

"Isn't that kind of like rumor-spreading?" Vicki asked.

"That's a good way of putting it. It's an intentional use of lies, spread for the purpose of changing the perception of truth. That's what Hitler used back in 1940, when he imposed his evil power on other nationalities in Europe.

"Part of Hitler's success was due to the fact that he used psychological warfare very effectively. He used frontline radio broadcasts and distributed leaflets behind enemy lines to spread untruths about his war machine. The German propaganda told how his unstoppable army would crush anything in its path. He bombarded the Allied troops with these lies to build fear in the soldiers' minds. Basically, Hitler waited for the 'psywar' to drain the fighting spirit from the opposition.

"Then, to capitalize on his campaign, he preceded his attacks with fast-moving rumors of total destruction in other parts of Europe and by the terrifying sounds of whistle-equipped dive bombers and fast-moving, terribly noisy armored personnel carriers.

"He built his campaign of lies until it had reached fever pitch. Allied troops nervously awaited the terrible onslaught they had heard so much about. In one case in the Western Campaign, Hitler planned to send the 35th Infantry Division to the Juliana Canal, the Meuse River, and the Meuse-Scheldt Canal. Once the division had taken these strategic passages, they planned to make a turn against the Albert Canal, a heavily fortified passageway. Those planning the attacks believed it would take at least five days to break through the Allied defenses because they were so heavily armed and had the luxury of huge bunkers, steep banks to hide behind, and heavy artillery with which to defend themselves."

The group was silent as they listened to Brad's story.

"If the Allied troops knew the truth of their situation, they would have courageously defended their position, because the truth was, they had a four-to-one advantage over the German army. But the whispering campaign had inflicted serious damage before the enemy had fired a single shot.

"What happened surprised everybody. Instead of taking five days to reach their first objective, they took the first position on the evening of the first day. The opposing troops offered very little resistance. In fact, soldiers either laid down their arms or took off running in retreat."

The group listened, their eyebrows raised. Obviously this hadn't been taught in their U.S. history classes.

"Then, check this out," Brad continued, animated with his passion for this story. "At a railroad crossing not far from the Canal, which was their main objective, a small motorized detachment of German troops arrived to face an incredibly well-reinforced Allied defense. But before they fired any of their heavy antitank guns, the Allies threw down their arms and retreated—laughing and waving because the war was finished for them before it had actually begun.

"Obviously, with that kind of behavior, the Allied resistance quickly collapsed at the Canal, too. And in no time at all, German engineers blasted gaps in the barbed-wire barricades and assault teams crossed the Canal. The Allies ceased firing and laid down their arms after only a few minutes."

Group members shook their heads with a combination of amazement and disgust.

Mike whispered, "Wow."

Ron said aloud, "That's incredible."

"What might have happened," Brad asked, "if the Allied troops had *not* been influenced by the lies of Hitler's whispering campaign?"

Mike said, "They could have kicked all those enemy hind ends right back to where they came from."

"Or better yet," Sandi said, "blown them right to a meeting

with their Maker. Just try explainin' *that* cause to God."

The others chuckled and Brad nodded in agreement. "The point of the story is this. When you are armed with truth, you possess a *powerful* weapon. And when that truth is the truth in God's Word, you have a shield of faith which allows you to act on what you *know* to be true. When you act on what you believe, there's no stopping you. Even Satan's fiery darts can't harm you."

Satan's Whispering Campaign Attacks God's Truth

"Let me put it this way," Brad continued, "when Satan tries to shoot the darts of untruth into our hearts, how we respond at that moment has more to do with what we believe about *God* than what we believe about ourselves."

"In other words," Ron interjected, "when we act on the truth in God's Word, we behave what we believe."

"That's a good way of saying it, Ron. *We behave what we believe.* I like that! And the more truth we add to our hearts by feeding our minds with Scripture, the stronger and thicker our shields get."

Mike said, "Cool!"

"We need to personalize this, though. Is someone willing to volunteer as an example, so we can apply this concept to impulse control?"

Sandi raised her hand.

"Good for you, Sandi," Brad said. "Now, you've told the group that you struggle with the urge to eat sweets. Is that right?"

"Yes, sir, it certainly is."

"Well, let me ask you, have you been able to identify some of the darts that tend to strike your heart just before you have the urge to eat?"

Sandi dug out one of her monitoring charts. "Yes, I have. The first week, all I knew was that when sweets were out on the table in the nurse's station, I'd look at 'em and get hungry. All it took was one look and whoo baby, I was ready for another brownie. After a couple of weeks of monitoring my urges, I made a discovery: I think my eating has more to do with anxiety than hunger."

"So you believe there's a link between your triggers and anxiety, is that right?"

"Oh yes, indeed, honey. Just about every time I'd get anxious, I'd see the chart go way up. I think I was eating to try to relieve my anxiety. Like they say, comfort food."

Brad responded, "It's quite common to give in to certain

urges because we're seeking comfort. We want to get rid of what we think is a bad feeling, so we simply find a substitute for that feeling—something that gives us a better feeling. But the way Satan works, he always tries to show us a shortcut. Instead of feeding us positive solutions that get to the heart of our problem, he'll give us a temporary solution that only winds up becoming another negative or destructive habit. So we wind up covering one bad habit with another bad habit."

"You can say that again." Sandi nodded.

"Sometimes, those comfort-seeking urges get us in trouble if they carry us into an extreme behavior. In your case, the extreme behavior is overeating. The fact that you seek some form of comfort isn't bad. But the fact that you repeat the same method of relief from anxiety over and over again, using food as the source of comfort, is what turns a good impulse into a destructive habit."

"Mmm-mmm-mmm," said Sandi, shaking her head in understanding. "And what I'm countin' on is *you* tellin' *me* how I can change this impulse, so I can find that comfort I'm looking for without eating so many confounded brownies."

Brad smiled. "That's exactly what we're going to learn next. I'll show you a couple of exercises that are *so* easy you may not believe it. You'll see how a couple of simple things can extinguish Satan's darts before they have a chance to ignite the embers in your heart. You'll see how easy it is to 'take captive every thought' and be obedient to Christ *before* your passions carry you away into destructive behavior."

"Well, let's get on with it, brother. I'm ready."

"Deal! Let's take another break to stretch. When we come back for our final thirty minutes, I'll show you a technique you can use to reverse the negative impulse process Satan tries to get started in our hearts."

Build a Skill

■ To reinforce what you've just learned about Satan's strategy to pull you into negative, destructive impulses, answer the following review questions.

1. What's the best defense against a fiery dart?

2. What's the best way to "construct" a shield of faith?

3. Satan's strategy is similar to Hitler's back when the German army used a certain type of campaign to gain an advantage over Allied troops. What is one name for this type of campaign?

4. What happens to our confidence when we begin to dwell on the lies Satan shoots into our hearts?

5. What happens to our ability to make courageous decisions when we know the truth about our situation, based on God's Word?

chapter nine

LOOKING AT BRICKS

The Flesh vs. the Spirit, Part 3

O kay, let's wind up our study with some of the most practical, effective tools you can use to beat Satan and turn those nasty negative impulses into positive ones," said Brad.

The Flesh ⟶ Rotten Fruit

"We know the enemy's strategy, and we know about his weapons. Now let's look at the results of our response to Satan's attacks. The apostle Paul uses an analogy of fruit to describe the two different types of results we can get from this impulse development process.

"The first type of fruit is what I call rotten fruit. This is what grows out of our lives if we allow our old sin nature to carry us into a negative, downward spiral of thoughts, feelings, and actions. Paul calls this type of behavior "walking in the flesh." When we walk in the flesh, we get the results described in Galatians 5:19–21, which are on the handout I put on your chairs during the break. Look at this list and see what kinds of actions Paul says result from walking in the flesh.

"You can see by that list—and it's *quite* a list—that when we allow Satan to defeat us with his whispering campaign, we forget the truth of God's Word and fall into some awful behaviors. Some of these are extreme and represent the behavior of someone who clearly is not living for the Lord. But look at numbers four and five. They may be more subtle but they're just as destructive. How many of us have struggled with one or more of these behaviors?"

ROTTEN FRUIT

1. Sexual immorality
2. Impurity and debauchery
3. Idolatry and witchcraft
4. Hatred, discord, jealousy, fits of rage
5. Selfish ambition, dissensions, factions
6. Envy, drunkenness, orgies

Everyone nodded or raised their hand.

"Satan knows it's more difficult to lead us astray all at once, so instead, he entices us away little by little, getting us farther and farther away from God's Word, until we have strayed farther away than we thought. I like to think of us as the Good Shepherd's sheep. The Shepherd is constantly trying to keep us under His watchful eye, but bit by bit, we can nibble ourselves away from the rest of the flock. One blade of grass at a time, we stray far enough away that we wind up falling off a cliff."

"Which," interjected Tom, "is why it's so important for me to keep feeding on the Word every day. I really notice that when I've not been nourishing my mind with God's Word, I have a lot more difficulty fending off Satan's attacks."

"Good point," said Brad. "The core truth about this whole impulse management thing is that when we choose to allow Christ to rule our hearts daily—moment by moment—then His Holy Spirit guides us through the process, giving us the strength to deflect the darts. The Holy Spirit is the one who turns each impulse into a God-honoring motivation to make the right choice and to do the right thing. That's why the Bible tells us that we can put off our old self as we walk in the Spirit and that we can be made new in the attitude of our mind."

The Spirit ⟶ Good Fruit

GOOD FRUIT

1. Love
2. Joy
3. Peace
4. Patience
5. Kindness
6. Goodness
7. Faithfulness
8. Gentleness
9. Self-control

"The good news is that when we renew our minds by walking in the Spirit, then we see evidence of the good fruit. These are the good outcomes Paul refers to as 'the fruit of the Spirit' in Galatians 5:22 and 23. Let's check out that list on your handout."

Vicki looked perplexed. "Uh, Brad? I've heard this term before, 'walking in the Spirit,' but what exactly does that mean?"

"Good question," Brad said. "It's easy for us to throw these terms around like everybody ought to know what we're talking about. I guess the best way for me to describe 'walking in the Spirit' is to tell you a quick story about a mountain climbing trip I took once."

Sandi said, "Oh good. I just love these stories. I can actually understand what you're talking about when you tell a story!"

So Brad launched into his tale. "Back when I was in college—and in much better shape than I am now—I went mountain climbing in the Colorado Rockies. It was a difficult climb, but the four of us in our group had a guide who had been to the top about a dozen times before. He knew what he was doing.

"About halfway up, I got a little cocky and thought I saw a quicker way around a group of rocks. I figured I would impress my guide by taking what I thought was a shortcut and beating him to the next plateau. But instead, I found myself stranded on a large, steep outcropping—where there was a lot of loose rock. It was really dangerous. It took about twenty minutes for my guide to notice I was missing and to hike back down and around to where I was stuck.

"With some simple instructions, he guided me with his voice to each new step, where I found solid ground and something to hang on to. In just five minutes I was safely back on the right trail, the one I should have stayed on in the first place."

"And boy, were you embarrassed," Mike offered.

"And boy, was I embarrassed," Brad echoed. "But to get to my point: Can you guess which person in this story stands for the Holy Spirit?"

"The guide," Vicki said.

Other heads nodded.

"Yep. To be 'walking in the Spirit' simply means that you allow Him to guide every step of your journey. Those who do that stay on the right trail. Those who try to do it their own way wind up getting off the trail, and they can really get in serious trouble. Those I know who are constantly walking in the Spirit don't just have a lot of Scriptures memorized; they don't just have a lot of knowledge *about* God. They walk *with* God, every day. In fact, every moment of every day. Their lives show an outward, visible demonstration that they are listening to the Spirit's voice."

Brad paused a moment to clear his throat. "They take seriously what the Bible says about letting God's Word 'dwell richly' in them. And because they are constantly walking with the Spirit, others continually see evidence of the good fruit growing out of their lives. It's that awareness that the Spirit lives inside their hearts and minds that allows those godly people I know to behave with such grace under pressure. They are able to act with self-control in situations in which many people would fly off the handle."

Sandi observed, "I've met some folks like that. It's amazing to see people who are walking in the Spirit. Now I understand why they can act that way. They're listening to the voice of their guide—the Holy Spirit of God Himself!"

"You've got it, Sandi," said Brad. "And this good stuff growing out of their actions is the 'fruit of the Spirit' the apostle Paul was talking about in Galatians. It's pretty obvious which type of fruit we would rather have growing out of our lives, right?"

Heads nodded yes. Sandi spoke for everyone: "Don't want no rotten fruit smellin' up *my* kitchen."

Brad couldn't help chuckling. "Then let me show you a wonderful tool that will enable you to pull yourself out of the downward spiral of negative thoughts that lead to the rotten fruit."

Take Every Thought Captive

Brad picked up his Bible. "The Bible reveals a powerful tool God makes available to us in our war against the flesh. Would someone please read 2 Corinthians 10:4 and 5?"

Ron quickly found the passage and read, "'The weapons we fight with are not the weapons of the world. On the contrary, they have divine power to demolish strongholds. We demolish arguments and every pretension that sets itself up against the knowledge of God, and we take captive every thought to make it obedient to Christ.'"

"Thanks, Ron. Can someone tell me what kind of fruit would grow out of our lives if we were to fight against Satan using our flesh?"

"Bad fruit," Kaycee said. "Rotten fruit."

"That's right. God's Word just told us that we can't use our flesh to fight battles with Satan, because when we do, we play into his hand. We wind up becoming just as ugly as the thing we are fighting against."

Vicki spoke up. "Yeah. Like when my kids get angry and I wind up yelling at them to stop being angry. It seems like I'm teaching them that it's only okay to scream and holler if you're an adult."

"Good insight, Vicki. And no matter what urge or impulse we're fighting, when we try to beat Satan by using the flesh, we're only heading down that negative spiral leading toward rotten fruit. But in the last portion of the passage Ron just read we find the solution. There's a powerful weapon we can use against the enemy. Can someone tell me what that weapon is?"

They scanned the passage again. Sandi asked, "Does it have to do with thoughts?"

Brad nodded. "And what *about* our thoughts?"

"Is it the part about taking captive every thought and making it obedient to Christ?"

"You got it, Sandi. You can take captive every negative thought *before* it grows into a negative impulse and *before* it turns into rotten fruit. Look at the steps I've given you in the handout, just under the two kinds of fruit."

"Say what?" exclaimed Mike. "Look at a brick? What's up with that?"

"I'm glad you noticed that. It's the practical tool I'm about to teach you how to use."

To Take Captive
Every Thought

1. Put on the mind of Christ by reading His Word. (When you do this, you are walking in the Spirit by letting the Word dwell richly within you.)

2. As you study His Word, ask Him to guide you into truth through His Holy Spirit. (He promises to do this in John 14:16, 17, 26; 15:26; 16:13, 15. Key verse: 16:13.)

3. When you get hit by a dart, look at a brick.

Look at a Brick

"I'd like you to think of each truth in God's Word as a brick. Can you picture a whole bunch of truths, all stacked on top of each other, forming a strong wall?"

They all pictured the thought in their minds and nodded.

"Now, as we build our shields of faith, what makes up the unburnable building material?"

"Truth from God's Word," answered Ron.

"Right. And so, instead of a small, wooden shield, we're

going to build a huge, nonflammable brick shield, big enough not only to stand behind, but big and strong enough to build a jail cell around the negative thoughts that come as a result of the fiery darts. Have you got that picture in mind?"

They nodded.

"Now I'm going to share one of my favorite verses for you to think about while I explain this Look at a Brick concept. I love Proverbs 30:5, which says, 'Every word of God is flawless; he is a shield to those who take refuge in him.' Isn't that amazing?"

"Exactly what we're talking about," Kaycee said.

"In that verse, who is the one doing the shielding?"

"God," they answered together.

"And what is it that is flawless?"

"His word," said Sandi.

"*Every* word," added Ron.

"Good. Now hold that verse in your mind as I pick one of you as my guinea pig—er, I mean, *example*—and demonstrate how you can take a thought captive by looking at a brick. Which one of you would like to volunteer?"

Awkward smiles. "I volunteer Mike," Sandi said.

"Yeah, good idea. Mike! Mike! Mike!" the group clapped and chanted.

Brad laughed. "Thanks for volunteering, Mike. I'm going to let you show the group how easy it is to take captive a thought, okay?"

"Let's go for it!"

"Now just relax and think of a time lately when you were really fighting some urge. Can you think of one?"

Mike looked a bit self-conscious, but blinked away his fear and closed his eyes for a moment while he thought. "Okay," he said, "I've got it."

"Let's see if we can get you to feel the same level of anxiety you felt in that moment. So why don't you describe for us, in the present tense, what it is you're doing, where you are, and why you are anxious."

"Well…" Mike shifted in his seat and stared straight ahead, as though looking at something. "I'm at work at the music store, and I'm helping a customer. I'm putting a new set of strings on his guitar when in walks this…"

He takes a deep breath, shakes his head like he's shivering, and then exhales fast and loud.

"In walks this vision. I could feel some of those body cues we've been learning about. My palms got sweaty, I could feel my face get warm. And I had a terrible time…well, uh, this is kinda embarrassing…"

Brad encouraged him. "That's okay, Mike. Remember the rules Tom went over at the very beginning of the group? Anything revealed here stays confidential. And if you think it's too personal to share, you can keep it general. You don't have to share anything you feel might embarrass you later."

Mike took another breath and said, "Okay. Thanks. Let's just say that I found myself fighting the urge to sneak peeks at this young woman, and it got so bad that I was afraid the customer I was helping would notice that I was more interested in her than in him."

Brad asked, "So you were really having a difficult time concentrating, and you were afraid the customer would notice that you were having impure thoughts?"

"That's a good way of saying it," said Mike. "I really tried not to let my mind wander, but it was pretty difficult."

"Mike, thanks for being honest with us," Brad said. "You're a brave man to admit to what most men struggle with from time to time."

The women looked supportive; the men looked sympathetic.

"Now, Mike," Brad continued, "in your mind's eye, put yourself in that time and place again and tell me how high on the thermometer your anxiety level is right now, at this moment."

Mike thought for a moment. Group members could see the anxiety on his face. "I'd say about an eighty or ninety. It's way up there. I mean, I know I tease a lot about liking girls and stuff, but I really do care about my Christian witness and I don't want people to think that's all I ever think about."

"I understand." Brad said. "Now Mike, I want you to look at the wall next to you, the one by the fireplace, and describe for me what you see."

Mike's expression showed that he wondered where this strange instruction was leading.

"It's okay. This will be painless, I promise. You are about to demonstrate something very simple, yet very powerful."

"Okay," said Mike, swiveling in his chair to face the wall. "I see a wall made of bricks, with a fireplace in the middle, and a mantle made of a rough beam over the top of the fireplace."

"Good. Now pick a small portion of that wall—about a square foot—and get more detailed. Tell me what you see."

"Ummm, I see about, oh, maybe ten or twelve bricks. They are different colors. Some are darker than others." He stopped as though that was all he could describe.

"More detail. Tell me more."

"Okay." Mike refocused on the same group of bricks. "There are some small cracks in a few of the bricks, and the mortar between each brick is sort of a gray color. Uh, and it looks like there are some little scrape marks in some of the bricks."

"Good. Now Mike, I want you to tighten your focus on just *one* brick. Pick any brick in the middle of that group, and describe what you see. Be as detailed as you can."

The group members watched as Mike's focus began to shift from anxiety over the situation he had described to intense concentration on the brick. Ron jotted a couple of phrases in his notebook.

"I see a rust-colored brick, mostly rectangular, but with a couple of edges that have been sort of chipped off. There is a small, jagged crack running through the upper right-hand corner, like a little river. And there are about three different colors in the same brick. The lighter colors are where the scrape marks are, and the dark color takes up most of the brick."

"Excellent," said Brad. "Now, I want you to feel your body cues. Tell me how high on the thermometer is your anxiety level at this moment?"

Mike's face changed from concentration to a grin. "Wow," he exclaimed. "I feel pretty darn good. I'd say it's down to about a ten or twenty. And only because I'm a little embarrassed about being the guinea pig."

The group laughed.

Brad said, "You've just done something that every one of us can do every time our fleshly nature starts a downward spiral of negative thoughts. You simply looked at a brick."

The light of recognition went on in the eyes of a couple of members.

"And I want you to notice something important, Mike," Brad continued. "Nobody touched you. Nobody forced you to do anything you didn't want to do. You exercised your will, and you simply refocused your attention on something other than the negative thoughts that were causing those feelings of anxiety. You have the ability to use this powerful weapon any time you want. Now, what emotion do you feel?"

Mike thought for a moment. "Relief. Optimism."

"Why optimism?"

"Because now I know how to keep from feeling so anxious about my impure thoughts. I can...take them captive," answered Mike.

Sandi cheered. The group applauded.

"Exactly. You can do that, Mike. Let me ask the rest of you: Instead of simply focusing on a literal brick, what can you direct your thoughts toward that will help you build a shield of faith and a jail cell to take captive negative thoughts?"

Another look of recognition beamed on Sandi's face. She exclaimed, "The truths from God's Word!"

"Exactly. Paul tells us in Philippians 4:8 that we should think about 'whatever is true, whatever is noble, whatever is right, whatever is pure, whatever is lovely, whatever is admirable,' and if anything is 'excellent or praiseworthy,' we should think about those things too. When you put on the mind of Christ by daily pouring His Word into your heart and mind, you store up a whole supply of bricks. And each time a dart starts you down the path of negative thoughts, you can simply bring to mind one of those truths—one of those bricks—and focus on it. In just a matter of seconds, your emotions go back down the thermometer, because you've arrested the thought and built a jail cell around it with your 'truth bricks.'"

Take every thought captive...
one brick at a time.

Ron said, "Like that verse in Proverbs. God's word is flawless, and when we have His words in mind, *He* becomes our shield."

Sandi clapped her hands together and shouted, "Glory halleluiah, I could just shout!"

"I think you just did," Vicki said, but she smiled as she said it and the group burst into applause again.

The Spirit Gives You the Bricks

Tom and Kaycee looked at each other, pleased with the breakthroughs the group was experiencing.

Brad, too, seemed delighted. "One more thing," he said. "Who guides you to the bricks? If I gave you each a set of Bible verses and told you to memorize them, it might help, but I can't guide you to the truths you need to store up in your mind. I'm inadequate for that task."

Ron spoke up. "On the handout it says that we can ask the Father to show us, through the Spirit. Several verses in the book of John are listed."

"And the key verse listed there is John 16:13: 'But when he, the Spirit of truth, comes, he will guide you into all truth,'" Brad said. "And who has access to the Spirit of truth?"

"All of us who have Christ in our minds and hearts," Mike answered.

"Minds *slash* hearts," Sandi clarified, good-naturedly.

"You can bank on it," said Brad. "When you are putting on the mind of Christ, you have access to the Spirit of truth. He will guide you into all the truths you need in order to store up a huge pile of bricks. And that's what I want you to do for your homework assignment this week."

Everyone prepared to jot down the assignment.

"I'd like you to choose one area you are struggling with. It's probably the one you've been charting these past few weeks. Then, each day, whenever you have your Bible reading and prayer time, I want you to begin with a simple prayer thanking the Father for giving you His Holy Spirit. Thank Him that Jesus promised you the Spirit of truth. Then, as you read through portions of the Bible, ask Him to guide you into the truths that will help you develop a shield of faith. Each time you read a verse or passage with a truth that counters the lies Satan is trying to deceive you with, write that passage down. If possible, memorize the key verse in the passage. You can journal it if you wish, by keeping a sheet of paper handy, so you can compile a whole list of 'truth bricks.'"

The members finished writing their instructions.

"And Tom, I'd like to thank you and Kaycee for inviting me to be part of this wonderful group. You guys are the greatest. I'm quite sure you folks are going to be walking in the Spirit, taking captive every thought. I'd love to come back in three or four weeks and hear some of your success stories. I always get a kick out of watching people win the battles over their impulses. Is there any chance we could meet again, just to hear how everyone's doing with these tools?"

"Let's do it," someone said. Others agreed, and they planned to meet again in three weeks for a final wrap-up party, complete with testimonies about how God was working in each person's life.

Build a Skill

■ Answer the following questions to review what you've just learned about taking captive every thought and making it obedient to Christ:

1. What is the material used in building your shield of faith?

2. What does it mean to "look at a brick" when you find yourself in a downward spiral of negative thoughts?

3. Where do you find the bricks you will pile up to make your shield and the "jail cell" for the negative thoughts you will take captive?

4. Who leads you to those truths?

5. What will you do this week to start piling up your bricks?

Part Two

∎

In part two, members of Tom's group present testimonials of how they are applying what they've learned about recognizing and overcoming negative emotions and impulses. Their stories reveal how they are learning to conquer anxiety, compulsive behavior, grief, anger, depression, overeating, dishonesty, overspending, fear, and lust—all of which had been keeping them from reaching their God-given potential.

If you are battling a negative emotion or impulse that does not happen to be mentioned above, don't skip part two! You will still find the group's stories to be helpful and encouraging—and you will pick up some practical suggestions that will help you apply the principles you learned in part one to your own situation.

chapter ten

THE COKE-CAN MOMENT

Anxiety Masked by Compulsive Behavior (Ron's Story)

T
HREE WEEKS LATER, in Tom and Kaycee's living room. The group has been applying the lessons they learned and have gathered for a wrap-up party to share how they're doing.

"Well, folks, it's our last hurrah," Tom began. The group stopped visiting and settled back in their seats. "Kinda sad to say good-bye, but we're really here to celebrate…"

"So let's eat," Sandi interrupted, laughing.

"Oh, we *will*," Tom said. "But not quite yet, Sandi. As you'll recall, we decided three weeks ago to reconvene tonight and share what God has done in each of our lives since we took the course. We want you each to tell how God has used these tools you've learned and are starting to master."

"Who gets to go first?" asked Vicki.

Ron raised his hand. "Since I'm the teacher's pet, I'll volunteer."

Vicki flashed him a sarcastic look but couldn't maintain it. Her face melted into a broad smile. "Well then, take it away, my friend."

"Is that okay? Should I start?" Ron looked to Tom.

Tom checked his watch. "Well, Brad was going to try to join us tonight, but he must have gotten held up or had a change of plans. So why don't you go ahead?"

Ron put his notebook on the floor beneath the coffee table and took a breath as he gathered his thoughts.

"What?" Vicki exclaimed, before Ron could get the first word out. "No notes? I thought you'd have a slide presentation or video or something."

Ron shrugged, then pointed to his head. "Got it all up here, Vicki."

Everyone laughed, then Ron launched into his testimony. "I'll start with a story to illustrate something that happened to me as a result of this course. I watched this movie on TV, *At First Sight,* just a couple of nights after our last meeting. It was the one about a man who lost his sight as a young boy and then finally regained it as an adult. It was a pretty good story, I thought. I wouldn't want my kids to see parts of it, but I watched it after they had gone to bed.

"In the movie, there was a powerful moment. It was when Val Kilmer's character was about to have his bandages removed after the surgery that gave him back his sight."

Sandi put her hands together, shook them up and down, and said, "Oh yes. Oh, my goodness."

"The operation worked," Ron continued, "and the man

could see, but…there was a major problem. He had lived in darkness for so long that his brain had no reference points for the images it was seeing. The bright lights were terribly frightening. The random colors were all a blur, and he was actually traumatized by the new sensations."

Sandi was visibly distressed. "I felt so sorry for him. It was terrible!"

"It *was* terrible," Ron added. "It was as though everyone expected him to suddenly see the same things they saw every day—and to know instantly what those things were. But it just didn't happen that way."

For once Vicki didn't wisecrack. "So what happened?" she asked.

"Well," Ron smiled, "my favorite scene in the whole movie was the Coke-can scene. The doctor handed Val Kilmer a can of Coca-Cola and said something like, 'Here, feel this and let your brain tell you what you're holding.' He took hold of the can, with his eyes still shut. He felt the can with his fingers for a moment, then opened his eyes. I'll never forget his response. It was great. He said, 'Oh, so *this* is a Coke can!'"

Sandi clapped her hands and shouted, "Yessss!"

"So, this changed your life…how?" Vicki asked.

"About three days after I saw that movie, I was going over my charts and something really powerful dawned on me. I had been studying my body cues, my emotion thermometer, and all the stuff we had covered just like a typical engineer would. You know, analytical and by the book. But something my wife had said to me before woke me up to something."

The group watched Ron, waiting for his next sentence.

"My compulsive behavior—the cleaning, the organizing, the categorizing—has been something I thought was a positive trait.

But it dawned on me that every time I felt anxious about something I thought I couldn't control, I would simply organize my way out of my feelings. The statement my wife had made before was, 'I don't want you to solve my problem. I just want you to hear how I feel. And I'd like you to tell me how *you* feel once in a while.'

"So one night I began reviewing the exercises we learned. I followed the chart we've been working with, starting with the triggers. I thought about the triggers that had brought about a higher-level intensity in my compulsive behavior. In order to uncover the emotions that were connected with these triggers, I began a search for certain emotions. I brought to mind certain pictures that helped me tap into memories of times when I had felt certain ways. Then I'd check for the intensity level of that feeling—"

"Sounds like an engineer to me," Mike said. "So methodical."

Ron smiled. "Compulsive, actually. And not so healthy, in my case. So when I estimated the intensity level of the feeling, I checked my body cues and outward behaviors. As I did so with several different emotions, I discovered something remarkable. It became quite evident with the feeling of anxiety. I had been so accustomed to covering over my anxious feelings with compulsive behavior that I failed to recognize what that emotion looked like or felt like. Suddenly, I had a Coke-can moment."

Faces brightened as though a light bulb had gone on above people's heads. Some heads nodded.

"It was as though I had been emotionally blind for a long time—and suddenly, I used these tools to tell my brain what different feelings felt like. When I finally recognized anxiety for what it was, it dawned on me and I said out loud: 'Wow, so *this* is anxiety!'

"What God did for me through that one insight was to give me the tools I needed to recognize certain feelings and the courage to explain to my wife how I actually felt. I had always been afraid she would think I was weak, or…."

He searched for the right word.

"Or maybe not as 'in control' as I've always projected myself to be. I hadn't allowed her to see my negative emotions or know how anxious I get over certain things, like deadlines or unexpected crises."

Kaycee spoke up. "But she probably respected you more for becoming open and vulnerable, didn't she?" She looked over at Tom, knowingly.

"That's exactly right," said Ron. "When I finally explained to her about my Coke-can moment, I did something I hadn't done in front of her in years. I actually wept as I explained some of my deeper feelings. And instead of thinking less of me, she—"

Ron's voice stopped short, and he paused a few seconds before trying again. "She hugged me and said, 'I've been waiting a long time for you to tell me that.'"

Tom glanced around the room. He was almost as surprised at Ron's revelation as was the rest of the group. Ron had never before revealed his emotional side in this way. But what surprised Tom even more was Vicki's reaction. She had grabbed a tissue from the end table and was trying to secretly dab the corners of her eyes.

Just seeing Vicki was almost enough to bring a lump to Tom's throat. Before he could commend Ron for sharing his discovery with the rest of the group, his wife spoke up.

Kaycee said, "Ron, I've got to tell you that I've always respected you for being a strong man of God and a highly organized leader. But I respect you even more for becoming real—to your wife and to the rest of us."

Ron's face flushed and, without speaking, he nodded to accept Kaycee's compliment. At that moment the doorbell rang, and Kaycee hopped up to see who was at the door. It was Brad.

When he walked into the room, the group gave him a standing ovation and applauded for a good ten seconds. Brad stood speechless for a moment, then motioned for them to sit down. "Man alive! I'm going to bring my wife and kids over here to take lessons from you guys. They don't ever give me welcomes like that."

After some incidental chatter, Tom filled Brad in on Ron's discovery, including a shortened version of the Coke-can story.

Brad said, "Great metaphor. Emotionally blind. A Coke-can experience. You were courageous to admit that to the group, Ron. Thanks. It's really powerful to see how God turns things we think of as weaknesses into strengths."

The group nodded their agreement.

"Can I ask one counselor-type question of you, Ron?" Brad added.

"Of course."

"I know it's been only three weeks since that last meeting, but you made your discovery about a week later, is that right?"

Ron nodded.

"Can you tell us if there are any other positive consequences of your discovery? Anything different happening, either at work or at home, because you are beginning to recognize other feelings and respond differently to them?"

Ron thought for a moment and then smiled. "Yes. One difference has happened, in a positive way. I have a couple of people who work for me, and I always thought they were sort of analytical like I am—or was—and so I always approached my relationship with them in a very businesslike way.

"But the other day, one of them—his name is Bill—mentioned in passing that his daughter was going to have her tonsils out. Normally I would have said something like 'Oh, I'm sure she's going to come through with flying colors,' and left it at that. But this time, I felt something and wasn't sure what it was, so I sort of mentally checked my body cues and had another Coke-can moment.

"I recognized that what I was feeling was anxiety. But it wasn't my *own* anxiety. I was feeling *Bill's* anxiety. I was feeling empathy."

Tom glanced over and noticed Vicki sneaking another tissue.

"I realize this may sound funny to people who are used to feeling empathy all the time, but for me it was like a brand-new experience. So instead of just passing off Bill's statement as I usually would have done, I asked him, 'How are you feeling about your daughter's upcoming surgery?'"

Brad said, "That was good, Ron. You were giving him a chance to express *his* feelings. What did he say?"

Ron laughed, but his laughter stopped short as his throat closed off from a rising lump again. "I'm sorry. I guess now that I'm starting to learn how to feel certain emotions, they're just going crazy. I'll have to learn how to keep from becoming a blubbering idiot."

Kaycee put a comforting hand on Ron's knee. "Oh Ron, you know we don't think that about you. It's really quite moving to see how God's been working in your mind and heart. Please go on."

"Well, Bill saw that I was genuinely interested in how he was handling this stress in his life, and he opened up and talked with me for about ten minutes. It was incredible. I don't think I'd had a ten-minute conversation with Bill about anything other than work—*ever.* It's like we connected on a whole new level. And I think his work is improving because now he sees that I really care about *him,* not just about how productive he can be. About him, as a person."

The group sniffled, applauded, and cheered Ron's breakthrough. Those on either side of Ron gave him quick hugs and pats on the back.

chapter eleven

THE TIP OF THE ICEBERG

Sadness and Grief Masked by Anger (Vicki's Story)

B rad had noticed Vicki's reaction to Ron's story.

"Vicki, you appear visibly moved by Ron's discovery," Brad said. He looked at her, waiting for a response.

She couldn't speak for a moment. When she found enough voice to talk, it was squeaky and quivering. "Well, for one thing, I never expected to see ol' Ronny break down like that." Vicki turned on Ron in mock anger. "How could you *do* that to me?" She grabbed for another tissue and tried to gain enough strength to speak.

Brad said, "It's okay, Vicki. Take your time."

She finally began, "I guess it's just that…well…hearing Ron talk about how he became aware of other people's feelings. That struck a nerve." She paused for a deep breath. "See, I realize that my anger kind of gives me an edge in most places. I've learned to use it to get what I want. But reviewing the Bible passages, and going through these exercises...."

Vicki paused again and looked at her Bible, fighting tears. "I think I've figured out where my anger comes from. It's not really what's deep in my heart. Actually, I'm just a scared little girl inside, but because my dad never treated me with anything resembling empathy, I learned to put up a tough front. I turned my anger into a wall of defense. He never seemed to want to listen when I would pour out my heart to him, especially if I was feeling sadness...or fear. He would always say, 'Go to your room if you're going to act like a crybaby. And when you can act tough enough to keep from crying, you can come back.' I guess I always thought his love was conditional. I figured that if I acted one way—the tough way—he would love me. But if I acted like I had any sadness or pain he wouldn't love me. So I learned to be a sarcastic, angry person. But not necessarily a person I like."

Brad probed a bit. "Vicki, that's an amazing insight. I'm curious: How did you figure this out—about your father, I mean?"

"Well, let's see," Vicki said, sitting up straighter. She looked more composed, because she was focusing on her observation instead of her emotion. "It was when I was charting those triggers that I made the connection. That and a kind of strange experience our family had with a puppy last week."

"A puppy?" Brad asked.

"Yes. See, I was beginning to figure out that my anger triggers were often related to how other men were treating me—or how I *perceived* they were treating me. They'd say things like 'C'mon, Vick, be a man' because I'd always tried to act tough like they were. Well, when they would treat me like that, I'd get really, really mad, and when I started trying to figure out what picture was in my mind at those moments—Tom, you know the freeze-frames you told us about?"

Tom nodded.

"I figured out that I was seeing my father, sitting in his over-stuffed chair, with his beer belly hanging out underneath the daily newspaper. I'd see that look on his face, the one he used to give me when he would tell me to go into my room if I was going to act like that."

"Like what?" Brad asked.

"Sad," replied Vicki. "Every time I tried to act sad, my dad sent me away. I was never allowed to act sad."

"You said something about a puppy?"

"Yes, that's when the dam finally broke and I had my own personal—" she looked over at Ron—"Coke-can experience."

Ron gave Vicki a look of empathy.

"My kids had been wanting a puppy for a long time, and I kept telling them 'No way!' because I figured it would be a mess and they wouldn't take care of it. All the typical excuses parents use to keep their kids from getting a pet. But finally I decided they were old enough, and my husband said 'They can handle a pet,' so I went with my two oldest to the dog pound to pick out a dog. I had heard that's the best way to get a dog. They're already 'broken in,' I thought, and they wouldn't be so little that you'd need to be up with them all night. Well, we found this dog, a mixed breed—"

Sandi said, "You mean a *mutt?*"

Instead of snapping back with a snide comment, Vicki said, softly, "Yes. A mutt. And it was so ugly it was cute, you know? Part golden retriever, part Australian sheepdog, and I think part Lab. And it was only about six months old. She acted so sweet around the kids. But I was still a little hesitant. Then one of my girls said, 'Why don't you hold her in your lap, Mom?'"

Sandi said, "Oh, sister, they *didn't!* The old why-don't-you-hold-it-Mom? trick."

"You're absolutely right, that did me in. I looked at those sad little puppy-dog eyes, and I tell you, I felt stuff inside I hadn't felt since I was a kid—when I had a puppy of my own. In fact, when my dad used to send me away when I was sad, I used to go out and hold my puppy."

Sandi closed her eyes and sighed. "Oh, child...."

Brad asked, "Did the new puppy lead you to the realization that your anger triggers were related to your childhood feelings?"

"Well, no, not exactly," Vicki answered. "It was actually what happened four days *after* holding the puppy that caused me to put two and two together. Unfortunately, the puppy—we named her Diamond because of a diamond-shaped white patch on her back—began showing some disturbing behavior shortly after we got her home. She was so gentle with our family, but when one of my daughter's friends came over one afternoon, Diamond started barking like crazy and acting like she was going to tear into the poor kid."

"Did your daughter's friend do anything to startle the dog?" asked Kaycee.

"No. That's what was so strange. We thought it was just a freak thing and that she would learn to accept our family's friends. But then a couple of days later, Diamond did the same thing with another little friend—this one even younger than the first. I had to literally hold my dog back by her collar. I was afraid she was going to chew up this poor, scared kid.

"We had a talk, as a family, and decided we had to take Diamond back to the pound."

Kaycee sighed, "Oh no."

Vicki said, "Oh *yes*. I knew it was the only thing we could do. My girls have friends over after school all the time, and we couldn't have the dog bite one of them. That one poor kid was so scared that she told my daughter she wasn't going to come over to our house as long as we had the dog there."

Tom asked, "So you took the dog back?"

Vicki's eyes grew suddenly wet. She nodded yes, and bit her lower lip. "I told myself, *You're acting silly. Why don't you grow up and act tough? This is ridiculous.* But because of the stuff I'd been studying, and because I was beginning to feel things I hadn't felt in a long time, I was pretty confused. I couldn't believe I had grown attached to this little animal in only four days. The night before we had to take Diamond back, I had kicked off my shoes after a long day in high heels and was lying on the couch, trying to sort through my body cues, listening to what my body was telling me about what I was feeling. And I finally decided…it was the emotion of sadness. I felt terribly, horribly sad. Something I hadn't felt in a really, *really* long time. And all of a sudden, I started to cry. And cry, and cry some more."

Brad asked, "Did this new feeling and its effect on you seem frightening at first?"

"Oh yeah. I was scared to death. I thought I was cracking up or something. I didn't know how to turn off the faucet. But then my husband hollered around the corner, asking me if I had done the white load of laundry because he was out of underwear. Something snapped inside, and I thought, *I'm finally having a good cry here—I'm feeling truly sad for the first time in years—and all you can think about is your stupid underwear!*"

Kaycee put her hand over her mouth. She almost chuckled, but she could see that Vicki was serious, obviously reliving the intense moment she was describing.

"I got up, went into the bathroom, grabbed a couple pair of his dirty underwear out of the hamper, threw them at him, and yelled, 'If you need clean underwear so badly, do them yourself!' And he just stood there, with this goofy look on his face, staring at me, stunned. He probably couldn't remember when he had seen me with tears running down my face like that."

"And how did you make the connection with the anger triggers and your father?" Tom asked.

"I decided I was just too sad to clean up the dinner dishes, so I went to the bathroom to brush my teeth. I intended to crawl into bed early and be sad for a while longer. But I was still so mad at my husband and his stupid underwear that I flung open the door to the medicine cabinet, which hit the clock on the wall, knocked it to the floor...."

"Oh honey." Sandi's eyes widened.

"The glass on the front of that stupid clock shattered, making all kinds of noise. I screamed a bad word—I won't repeat it, but trust me, it wasn't pretty—and I stood there, not knowing which way to turn since I was in my stocking feet with glass all over the place. And then I heard Diamond's little paws scurrying over the kitchen floor, heading toward the bathroom. The noise must have gotten her attention."

Sandi put both hands over her mouth.

"I just knew that if the dog came running in to see what had happened, she would cut her little feet, so I made a mad dash for the door to shut it..."

Kaycee cringed.

"...and stepped on the glass myself."

Sandi groaned. Kaycee said, "Oh my." Even the men winced as they imagined the pain.

"I hollered again, the same bad word—even more loudly

this time—and just stood there, not moving, wondering what in the world to do next."

"What *did* you do?" asked Sandi.

"I took a few deep breaths to calm down, and—you're not going to believe this—I remembered to look at a brick."

Tom grinned and looked at Brad, who returned one that said, *Aha!*

"I settled down and calmly asked my husband if he would be so kind as to put Diamond in the basement, then get a broom, dustpan, and the kitchen trash can and sweep up the glass from the bathroom floor while I tended to my feet."

"How badly did you cut your feet?" asked Kaycee.

"Not very bad, really. Only a couple of shallow cuts. Nothing serious. Some disinfectant, two Band-Aids, and a good night's sleep, and I was fine."

Then, remembering where she was going with her story, Vicki said, "Oh yes, the connection with the triggers! As I lay in bed that night, trying to process what had happened, some of those earlier memories came flooding into my head. I remembered thinking, *If only I could let some of this sadness out.* In my mind, I saw my dad sitting in that stupid old chair of his, and I remember feeling like my emotional dam was about to break. But I had learned to stuff those sad feelings way down deep and cover them over with a thick slab of anger. And then something else hit me." She nodded toward Ron. "This was my Coke-can experience."

"What was that?" asked Brad.

"The next day, as I drove over to the dog pound to return Diamond, it hit me like a ton of bricks. *I* was like Diamond."

Silence. Rapt attention.

Vicki continued, "I figured someone must have hurt

Diamond, someone close to her, probably her previous owner or one of the owner's kids. My daughter's friends must have reminded Diamond of the person who had hurt her in some way. I don't know this for sure, but it seems to make sense. And I figured that it wasn't her fault she had developed such vicious, angry behavior. She couldn't help the way she had been treated before. Just like I couldn't help the way I was treated by my dad."

Vicki's last two statements were strong, resolute, confident.

Now it was Kaycee who reached for a tissue.

"But I figured, *I'm a human being, not a puppy dog,*" and with that, Vicki began to tear up again. "And I thought about that brick I had looked at—the Psalm that assures me I am 'fearfully and wonderfully made.' And I thought of another verse, Psalm 34:18: 'The LORD is close to the brokenhearted and saves those who are crushed in spirit.' Then I thought about the story in John, how Jesus wept after his friend Lazarus had died. And I thought, *Diamond might not be able to figure out what to do with her behavior. But I can.*" And with that, Vicki began to weep, her shoulders visibly shaking.

"It's okay, Vicki. You're doing great." Brad said.

"Take your time, hon," Sandi added.

"Well," Vicki said, openly crying without apology, "I got the dog into the pound and asked the lady at the front desk if I could take her back to her pen. She said yes, and I got Diamond all the way back there, and as soon as I shut the door to her cage I began to cry. I allowed myself to feel sad—really, truly sad." She sobbed in front of the group.

Kaycee, who was also crying, got up, walked over to Vicki, leaned over and hugged her. Vicki let her. Sandi joined them, and the three women cried together for a long moment. "Thank you," Vicki whispered.

Everyone was visibly moved.

Brad said, "Vicki, you might be encouraged to know that lots of women deal with the type of stuff you just described, and many of them don't make the kind of breakthrough you have made. You've done two things really well. First, you recognized the source of your anger triggers. Some people take a long time to figure that out. And second, you made a decision *not* to be controlled by your past. You've decided to allow God to control your emotions, through His Holy Spirit. And you've decided not to blame your dad for your behavior, now that you're an adult. That's incredible. I'm really proud of you."

Vicki's face tightened up like she was going to cry again. "My dad never told me that. He never once told me, 'I'm proud of you.'" And she wept a bit more before saying, "Thank you, Brad."

She was also able to thank the group. "You guys have seen a side of me not too many others have seen...yet. But they're going to. The old nature is giving way to the new creature I'm becoming in Christ. And by golly, some folks are going to see a new Vicki."

The group burst into applause again.

Brad couldn't resist the urge to seize the teachable moment. "Vicki, you've just demonstrated something important for the rest of us. If you could picture an iceberg, with the top sticking out of the water, and if you could label the part you could see *Anger*, then you'd get a picture of what happens to many of us. We often only see the anger, but underneath the surface are several other layers, all bigger than the first, so that the unseen foundation of that anger may be something very different."

He pulled out a legal pad and began sketching as he talked. "Most of us find it difficult to deal with unpleasant emotions—

like anxiety, for example. So we learn to cover up that emotion with our all-purpose emotion."

Brad turned his pad around for all to see.

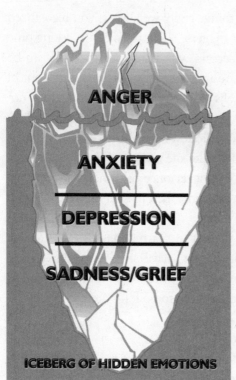

ANGER

ANXIETY

DEPRESSION

SADNESS/GRIEF

ICEBERG OF HIDDEN EMOTIONS

"Anger," Vicki said. "Yep. That's me."

"And it's often very frightening when we tap into the lower layers of those emotions. When we can peel away each layer, starting with anger, we may not like how we feel, but it's okay to feel that way. It's okay to feel anxiety, and even deep sadness, because we all grieve. Vicki, you pointed out that even Jesus cried, so we know *He* must have felt these emotions, too."

She nodded.

"You've done some very hard work—discovering how to allow certain emotions can be very difficult—but it's obvious you have already begun to see the benefits. The Holy Spirit is redirecting your thoughts, feelings, and actions as you recognize the emotions God gave you. And you have made a commitment to keep renewing your mind with His Word. Good job!"

"You go, girl," Sandi added. And the group applauded again.

chapter twelve

THE BREAD
OF LIFE

Depression and Anxiety
Masked by Overeating
(Sandi's Story)

ell, since Vicki has done such a good job," Sandi said, "I don't feel quite so shy about telling my story. I'll go next."

"You, *shy?*" Mike said.

"Oh honey, you've just seen the tip of *this* girl's iceberg. There's lots of stuff under the surface, and I'm only just now discovering what it is."

Brad said, "Good for you, Sandi. What *have* you been discovering during the past three weeks?"

"Well, first off, I have discovered that you are absolutely right about that anxiety thing. I *hate* the feeling of anxiety. Makes me feel like my skin is crawling. And that's what was behind my eatin' all those brownies at work. I'm convinced that I've got an anxious gland, and it's connected to my right arm. 'Cause every time I'd get anxious, that old arm will reach right on out there for those brownies and such."

The group laughed.

"But I've got some good news. Not great news, but good news. I've lost three pounds in the last three weeks."

"What was the turning point, Sandi?" asked Tom. "How have you applied these tools to help you conquer the urge to snack?"

"Well, it's funny. I guess I was still trying to figure out how to put all this together when my daughter, Sasha, taught me a lesson that made our class sort of click into place for me. About a week before we finished the course, she started crying at night when I'd tuck her in bed. She kept sayin' she was sad, but she couldn't figure out why. I asked her if there was someone treating her bad at school. She says no. I asked her if she felt sick. She says no. This went on for two nights in a row. Finally, on the third night, I thought about the pictures in your mind being memories, so I asked her, 'Sasha? When you get sad, honey, what picture do you see in your mind?' I didn't know if she would know what I was talking about, but I asked her, just in case. And you know what?"

"What?" three people asked simultaneously.

"She says, 'Fluffy.' Fluffy was her pet hamster that died a few months ago. I thought, *That's strange that she would still be cryin' over a dumb little hamster.* Especially since it had been months since it died. But then I remembered some of the stuff we had studied, about emotional imprints and negative feelings being stirred up when we see certain pictures in our heads. So I asked her, 'Honey, what do you see when you see Fluffy in your mind? Describe it for me.'

"She said, 'I see him in that little basket you fixed for him when he got sick, Mama. And he's breathin' real hard, and he's making that little squeaking sound 'cause he's got pneumonia and he's gonna die.'"

Kaycee's face revealed that she was feeling Sasha's sadness. "What did you tell her?"

"Well, it's funny, because I had been goin' over my notes from the course, and I remembered how we can replace the negative pictures in our minds with positive ones, because those new thoughts make new emotions. So I said, 'Honey, I'm sorry Fluffy died, too. It makes me sad to think about it. And it's okay to feel sad.' But then I tried some of the stuff we've learned. I asked her, 'Can you remember a time when you and Fluffy had a great time together?' She said she did, so I asked, 'What time was that? Can you tell me what Fluffy was doing when you had a good time?' She said, 'Yeah, Mama, he was standing up on his back feet, with his little nose twitching, and he was in the middle of the living room floor waiting for me to pick him up and put him in his cage.'"

Tom checked the faces of all the group members. All appeared to be following Sandi's story closely. Tom smiled to himself and refocused on Sandi.

"I asked Sasha to tell me what had happened that day with Fluffy, so she could concentrate on the happy memory."

"That was a great way to handle it, Sandi," Brad said. "Sounds like you were doing all the right things. I'm glad you told her it was okay to feel sad. Sometimes we try to tell kids to think about something happy, but we don't allow them to feel sadness. That can be a mistake. You handled this situation very well."

"Thanks. It was funny. The more she described her fun day with Fluffy, the more you could tell she wasn't feeling sad anymore. But then, she got to the part in her story where she forgot to close the cage door and Fluffy escaped. So when Sasha came back to the living room the cage was empty. I remember how frantic she became when she couldn't find her hamster.

"'Don't worry, honey,' I had told her, 'we'll leave the cage door open and we'll put some of Fluffy's food here on the living room floor. I'll just betcha he'll come right back lookin' for it when he's hungry. He'll show up again.'"

Kaycee blurted out, "And did he come back?"

Tom laughed. "Of course he did, honey. Otherwise he couldn't have gotten sick, and Sandi couldn't have put him in that basket before he died."

"Oh, yeah," Kaycee said, a bit embarrassed. "I was so into Sandi's story that I forgot about the basket part."

"I *am* sort of skipping around a little," Sandi said. "Anyway, at the end of that day, sure enough, right when Sasha was getting ready to head to the kitchen for a snack, she heard this little noise and turned around. There was Fluffy, standing up, just as my little girl had said. He looked like he was saying, 'Okay, I'm done lookin' around now. Somebody pick me up and put me back in my cage. I'm hungry.'"

Kaycee smiled. Others did, too.

Sandi continued, "I told Sasha, 'The next time you start thinking those sad thoughts because you're thinking about the picture of Fluffy in the basket, you just think about the happy picture, like the one you just described for me. You just think about Fluffy standing up on his back legs that way and about the great times you had that day. And then try to remember other great times you had together and keep thinking about those happy pictures.'"

"What did she do after that?" asked Vicki.

"She smiled, kissed me good-night, and then started to drift off to sleep. When I walked by to check on her about five minutes later, she reached up and grabbed my hand. She said, 'Mama, I'm thinking of some more happy pictures.' And her eyelids were almost shut. In about two more minutes she was out like a light. No more crying."

"Oh, Sandi, " Kaycee said. "That's so touching!"

Tom glanced over at Vicki, expecting a sarcastic comment. Instead, Vicki smiled and nodded in agreement.

Brad asked, "Sandi, how did your daughter's experience bring *you* to a point of personal discovery?"

Sandi thought for a moment. "Well, I had been feeling some anxiety that week, mostly because work was stressful. Then my husband, Claude, who's a policeman, had been on some stakeouts, and I had been pretty worried about him. I was kind of lonely and scared for him and had been trying to avoid those bad feelings, and I kept feeling those urges to go eat something sweet. Comfort food, you know?"

Kaycee nodded, "Yes. I know. I *know.*"

"But then, after I saw what an instant change the 'happy pictures' had made on Sasha, I went to the kitchen table. But instead of grabbing a bag of cookies, I got my Bible and started looking for some bricks—you know, verses that would help me take those anxious thoughts captive.

"The more I read, the more bricks I found. I added several to my pile that night. And each time I'd start to feel anxious, I'd have those bricks all written out on a piece of notebook paper. I've kept that paper, and a couple of new ones, inside the cover of my Bible so I can keep adding more bricks. For me, the bricks help me concentrate on the 'happy pictures' instead of focusing on the scary ones that cause me to feel terrible."

"Can you tell us some of the verses you found?" asked Ron.

"Sure." Sandi quickly found the paper inside her Bible. "This one's my favorite: Philippians 4:6 and 7. 'Do not be anxious about anything, but in everything, by prayer and petition, with thanksgiving, present your requests to God. And the peace of God, which transcends all understanding, will guard your hearts and your minds in Christ Jesus.'"

"All *right!* That Scripture is one of my bricks, too!" Kaycee said.

"And it's my favorite Scripture passage these days," Sandi went on. "It reminds me that when I'm starting to feel anxious, I can look for—and find—lots of things to be thankful for. Like when I'm gettin' all worked up thinking about Claude tryin' to arrest some drug pusher with a gun, I start reciting and thinking about those verses.

"Another verse, Psalm 91:11, tells me, 'For he will command his angels concerning you to guard you in all your ways.' I think about that verse and I start thanking God: 'Thank You, Lord, for sending Your angels to guard my husband.' I can actually pray for my husband, and I can do it with thanksgiving. That verse gives me my own 'happy picture.' I start to concentrate on God's angels surrounding my husband and his partner, and I thank God: 'Lord, thank You that You are the Rock and a Mighty Fortress. Thank You that You are a Strong Tower. I pray You'll surround my husband with Your strong hand, and with Your powerful angels. Thank You for saving him. Thank You for protecting him. Thank You that You are more powerful than anything.'"

"*You* go, girl!" This time it was Kaycee's turn to commend Sandi.

Sandi continued, "So now I replace those negative thoughts that made me feel so scared, so anxious, that I'd want to eat all the time. I replace them with pictures of Claude being safely guarded and protected by God and His angels. And the peace that passes all understanding is guarding *my* heart and keeps *my* mind from runnin' away with terrible thoughts.

"Now, instead of getting hungry for physical food—which for me is a substitute for spiritual comfort—I reach for spiritual food. There's a verse that talks about that, too. I found it that first night after I tucked Sasha into bed. Jesus says, 'I am the Bread of Life. He who eats of this bread will *never* go hungry.' That's John 6:35, I think. So now I'm learning to allow the Holy Spirit to guide me to the real food, God's Word, the Bread of Life, instead of that nasty ol' sweet stuff that used to satisfy only for a few minutes."

As they had done for Ron and Vicki, the group applauded Sandi.

Then she held up her hands to silence the room. "One more thing," Sandi said. "Brad, I think your iceberg illustration applies to me, too. Except that for me, the tip of the iceberg wasn't anger, it was *overeating*. Under the surface were those other layers—fear, anxiety, and a feeling of helplessness since I can't be there to physically protect my husband when he's out on the job."

"That's a very astute observation," Brad said.

Mike said, "Astute. Is that good?"

Everyone cracked up. "Yes," said Brad, smiling. "It's very good."

chapter thirteen

DIVING INTO DEBT

Overspending and Dishonesty Masked by Depression (Becky's Story)

Brad, I've got this friend...."

It was Mike, speaking up just as everyone was settling in from a break. He stopped short and glanced over at Vicki, suspicious of what she was probably thinking. But Vicki just smiled back at him.

Mike continued, "I know, I know, it sounds like I'm talking about myself, but I'm not. I really *do* have a friend, someone who comes into my store all the time. He's been fighting a problem with overspending. What should I say to him? Can this stuff we've been learning help someone with that kind of problem?"

Brad thought for a moment. "It sure would, Mike. The best thing would be for your friend to take a course like this one, or perhaps you could steer him toward a Christian counselor or a

Christian financial counseling agency that specializes in helping overspenders. But...there is one couple I worked with in another state, before I moved here. Maybe if I told about their situation—without breaking any confidences, of course—you could pick up on some ways to apply these tools to that specific urge. Is there anyone here who *doesn't* struggle with overspending, at least occasionally?"

No hands went up.

"Go for it," Mike said. "It might even buy me a few more minutes before I have to talk."

"Well, this couple—I'll call them Becky and Bob—came to me for help after Bob discovered that Becky had run up their credit cards. *Way* up. In fact, we're talking a $20,000 debt just on credit cards—not to mention their mortgage, two car payments, and a fairly expensive lifestyle."

Members of the group grimaced at the thought.

"I taught both Becky and Bob how to use the same tools you guys have learned. They began charting their urges and emotions, and it turns out that Becky's 'tip of the iceberg' was spending. When some people avoid anxiety or sadness, they eat. Others turn to alcohol or drugs to cover negative feelings. Others turn to sex, because of the illusion of comfort and stress reduction. But in Becky's case, she went shopping and bought things she thought would make her feel better. Whenever she felt anxiety, she spent money. It gave her a temporary feeling of security, but it was false security. She felt good for a little while, but when she received the bills in the mail, reality hit hard."

Kaycee asked, "But how in the world could she build up *that* much debt?"

Brad smiled. "Easily. The same way a person can put on an extra twenty pounds, if eating is their false fix. A person who spends money to feel secure can rack up an impressive debt. She developed that terribly dangerous habit of taking out a cash advance from one credit card in order to make the payments on another card."

Tom said, "Ooh. That hurts."

"You're not kidding," said Brad. "Since the interest rates on cash advances are much higher than even the lending rate—which is already sky high—the new monthly balance on each card soared to the limit within just a few months."

"But what was she spending all this money on?" asked Kaycee, still in shock over the amount Brad was talking about.

"You name it. Clothes. Shoes. Eating out. She would offer to pay for her friends' lunches just to make her feel better and more well-liked by them, because she desperately sought acceptance. It's amazing how quickly those restaurant tabs can grow."

Sandi added, "Tell me about it. My husband and I had to cut up our credit cards about five years ago, for the same reason. We had only run up about $5,000 in debt, not twenty. But that eatin' out business will kill ya."

Brad continued Becky's story. "When we started identifying the other layers of emotion beneath the top layer, Becky discovered that she had really been avoiding a negative emotion of fear—mostly fear of rejection. It started with some patterns she developed when she was quite young. She figured out that if she gave her father gifts, he responded with hugs and kisses, and she felt accepted. She translated those patterns into her marriage. She misread some of Bob's anxiety signals when he would look at their finances, and she was afraid he wouldn't accept her if she wasn't contributing to the household kitty. So she worked real hard to earn extra money but fooled herself into thinking she was making him feel better by buying extra stuff."

"You mean she would buy things for him, too? Not just for herself?" asked Kaycee.

"Oh yes, she would buy him gifts all the time. Little things that she thought would make him think she was earning a lot of money. She was actually learning to lie to herself. She kept thinking, 'I'll earn a little more next month and pay off this card.' Pretty soon the lie grew to be really distorted, and she was living out a fantasy that would never come true. She would think, 'I'll work extra hard, and they'll give me a raise, and then I can afford to pay off this stuff and buy Bob some more presents. Then he'll accept me.'"

"That sounds tragic," said Kaycee.

"It was, believe me. The whole deception—the lie Satan tried to get her to believe—created this black hole where all her money was going. Pretty soon she was lying not only to herself, but also to Bob. She wasn't able to make a car payment, but she told him all the bills were paid. She kept saying to herself, 'What he doesn't know won't hurt him. I'll get it fixed next month.' But next month was always worse than the month before."

Tom asked, "How did Bob find out about it?"

"Oh, that was the hard part. Since Becky handled all the family's finances, he hadn't seen how bad things were getting. All he saw was what she wanted him to see—the gifts, the new clothes, new items around the house—and he thought everything was just fine. Until..."

Sandi took a deep breath, waiting for the bad news.

"Until she couldn't make about three house payments. One day Bob got to the mailbox before Becky did and found a foreclosure notice."

"Oh my goodness," exclaimed Sandi.

"It was quite a shock, as you can imagine. On top of the sudden financial worries, Bob lost trust in Becky because there had been so much deception."

Kaycee almost couldn't believe her ears. "But why couldn't she just level with him about how things were going?"

"Well, part of the reason is that Bob had a pretty volatile temper. And when he felt anxiety about money, he would get angry. Becky was so afraid of his reaction and so desperate to have his acceptance, that she created her own fantasy world and lived in it until the house came crashing down around them."

"Did they survive? I mean, their marriage?"

"Believe it or not, yes," said Brad. "It took about six months of intense marital and financial counseling, and lots and lots of patience, but they hung in there. I handled the interpersonal stuff, and they sought help from a Christian financial counseling agency that helped them with the practical aspects of digging out of debt. In my work with them, Bob demonstrated that he was willing to change his behavior related to his anger and accept Becky as she was—even if she could no longer buy him gifts. He needed to reassure Becky that he loved her and accepted her, regardless of their financial situation. And Becky learned what was behind her overspending and how to deal with it on the various levels. And that it was okay to be honest with Bob about their finances, even if it meant saying no to things."

"Good grief, man," said Mike. "That would have been a tough one to work through."

"It was." Brad shook his head. "They had to move into the basement of some friends' house for a month while they looked for a rental, and Bob had to get an extra job. It was tough on both of them. But you know what? They have grown so tremendously as a result of their trial that you'd hardly recognize the old couple. They are *both* new creations in Christ. And they are both learning to be content in their circumstances, without having to surround themselves with 'stuff' that gives the illusion of success."

Tom said, "I can sort of relate. To Bob, I mean. Because of my anger. I can see how easy it would be to get really mad if the finances got messed up."

"Anger is a pretty common problem," Brad agreed. "In fact, a huge percentage of the men who come to me do so because of a problem with anger. That's usually the surface indicator of a deeper problem."

"What was Becky's major symptom, besides the financial situation?" asked Kaycee. "What did she come to you for help with first?"

"Well, Becky was fairly typical of women who seek counseling. About 80 percent of women who come for help have some pretty obvious signs of depression at first. That's what Becky sought help for."

"What kinds of signs?" asked Sandi.

"Well, her symptoms were like many others I see; her sleeping habits changed—for a while she couldn't sleep much of the night, then she wanted to sleep all the time. She also noticed a pretty drastic change in weight. With depression, that change can be either up or down. Some gain weight, some lose it. With Becky, it was a pretty drastic gain in weight. That startled her enough that she wanted to find out why. She reported that she felt dull, listless, unmotivated. She couldn't even cope with daily routines, like doing laundry."

Sandi laughed. "Who can?"

Others laughed too. Brad said, "That's true. Laundry's hard to keep up with as it is. But in Becky's case, she just sat in the middle of the floor in her laundry room one day and started crying. She didn't even have the motivation to fold the clothes that were already clean."

Again Sandi said, "Who does?"

Brad continued, "Those were some of the classic signs that she was in depression. And it was good that she sought help, because serious, clinical depression is usually caused by more than just dirty laundry."

Sandi and Brad exchanged smiles.

"As I suspected, there was a lot more than just dirty laundry underneath the depression. As we uncovered the layers of urges and emotions that had built into her behavior, including the spending—which, as you can imagine, only added to her depression—we found something important. Becky made some very important connections between her behavior toward her husband and how she had behaved around her father—who had been a very angry, controlling person. She was acting toward Bob in the same way she had acted when growing up. For her, the Coke-can experience—I love that term, by the way—was when the light of recognition went on above her head, and she was able to acknowledge, 'My husband is not my father.'"

"Wow," exclaimed Vicki. "I think I can relate to that one."

"Yes. It's amazing how many women make that same discovery. It's a part of the Spirit-controlled life that allows us to become new creations, putting the past behind us and looking to the future He gives us."

"What were some of her 'bricks'?" asked Tom.

"Well, let's see," said Brad. "It's been quite a while since I worked with them, but I might be able to recall a couple of verses they mentioned. Oh yes, I remember one—Becky said she really clung to Matthew 6:31 through 33, where Jesus says,

'So do not worry, saying, "What shall we eat?" or "What shall we drink?" or "What shall we wear?" For the pagans run after all these things, and your heavenly Father knows that you need them. But seek first his kingdom and his righteousness, and all these things will be given to you as well' (Matthew 6:31–33). That whole passage about not worrying and how God cares for us was a real solid brick for Becky."

"I've got that one written down in my brick pile, too," said Sandi, "except I underlined the part about the food!"

"That's funny," added Vicki, "because I've got that one in my notes too, but the verse was important to me because it showed that my heavenly Father accepts me and cares for me."

Brad chuckled. "See how wonderfully personal the Holy Spirit is? He led you all to the same verse, but it had individual meanings for you because He knows your unique needs."

"I'm curious, Brad," Ron said. "Have you heard from Bob and Becky lately? Do you know how they are doing financially?"

"Actually, I got a Christmas card from them last December, and they wrote that in the five years since they started counseling, they had paid off all but $4,000 of their debt."

The group cheered.

"They also said that they planned to rent for one more year to pay off the rest of their credit-card debt and one of their car loans, and then they might be in a position to start looking for a house to buy. Only this time they will look for one within their means."

"It must have been a long road for them," said Kaycee.

"It was," said Brad. "You know the old saying as well as I do: 'Dive into debt; crawl back out.' That's what they did. They've been crawling for over five years, but they're about one year away from completely conquering it. And their marriage has survived some incredible stress."

"This stuff really works," Tom said.

"What do you mean?" asked Brad.

"This stuff," Tom replied, holding up his notebook. "These tools. The impulse development process. Letting the Holy Spirit guide you to the right verses which become the bricks. All of it. I get really excited hearing these stories. This stuff really works!"

chapter fourteen

WANT A BROWNIE?

Fear and Anxiety
Masked by Lust
(Mike's Story)

When Tom said that, others in the group nodded their agreement. "But the key," Tom continued, "is the Holy Spirit. He's the one who really does the work in this process. All the tools are good, but they are just ways to cooperate with Him."

"I'm glad to hear you say that," said Brad, "because that's the most important point in this whole course. Even if you forget every one of the tools you've learned, you'll still be okay if you just remember to trust the Holy Spirit and let Him guide you. *He's* the key to impulse control."

There was a lull in the conversation for a moment and everyone looked at Mike, who grinned sheepishly.

"I guess I'm next, huh?"

"Go for it," said Brad.

"Well, as you've probably already guessed by now, the peskiest urge I've been dealing with has to do with, uh, the opposite sex." Mike blushed a little. "And being a single guy, it has gotten to be pretty tough at times. But I'm really glad I've taken this course because I've learned some things that have already made a difference in my life. When the mental pictures start cranking up my urges, I'm learning to focus on other things. I'm not nearly as distracted as I used to be."

Brad asked, "Is there one specific tool that has helped more than the others?"

"Well, several of them are helping. Charting my urges, for one. And learning how to use the emotion thermometer, so I can tell how intense my feelings or urges are. But the real breakthrough for me happened when I was looking through a list of emotions. I was trying to figure out what emotions I felt when I started feeling those, uh, I guess you could call them 'lustful' urges. I made a discovery kind of like Ron did, except that my Coke-can experience wasn't recognizing a specific emotion. It was recognizing the difference between an emotion and an urge."

"Tell us what you mean by that."

"Well, when my brain finally clicked into gear, and I figured out what I was feeling, I thought, *Oh, so that's an emotion!* I had confused the urge called lust with the emotion of anxiety. And they were two different things."

Brad nodded.

"And, kind of like Vicki, I learned that the emotions of fear and anxiety were so scary that I didn't want to feel them. So instead, I covered over them with these urges."

Tom asked, "What things were you afraid of that made you so anxious?"

"Um, would you believe…women?"

Brad didn't laugh because he could tell Mike was serious. "I *can* believe that, Mike. It's pretty common for men to become anxious when they are around women. Especially when there is a physical attraction involved. They can be both attracted and afraid at the same time—two very conflicting emotions. And it's hard to figure out what we're feeling when we are experiencing two very different emotions at the same time."

"Well, that's exactly what was messing me up. I couldn't figure out what I was feeling. I just figured I had a problem with lust. It's made me feel a little better to know there's more to it than that."

A look of recognition swept across Mike's face. "Oh yes, I also figured out something about the triggers."

"What's that?"

"It's weird, but I noticed in my charting that I became more distracted when attractive women walked into my store if they were wearing the color red. So that's when I have to really concentrate on looking at a brick, when a woman in red walks in."

"That's not weird at all," said Brad. "I once counseled someone who had a strong emotional imprint when they were young, and the person they were attracted to was wearing blue at the time. This person generalized that trigger, and all he had to do was see a blue car drive up in his driveway and all kinds of feelings would start happening. It's more common than you might think. The good thing is that you recognize it, so you can be proactive and take those thoughts captive."

"Yeah. I wish I could say that I've conquered it once and for all," Mike said. "But it's such a struggle."

"And it probably will be. But walking in the Spirit is a moment by moment process, not a one-time quick fix. Some people may struggle with a certain impulse their entire lives, but they can still have victory by renewing their minds through the Word of God and walking with the Spirit of God. His strength is sufficient."

Tom said, "Brad, if I can add one thing here? One thing that's helped me in managing my anger impulse is remembering that when I do slip—and we all do—I can do something about it. I'm not locked in to helplessness, not doomed to perpetual misery. I can identify that I've sinned, repent from that sin, and confess it to God. The instant I do that, He forgives. I can then put that sin aside and continue the process of renewing my mind.

"Isn't it great that God isn't a one-strike-you're-out God? He is always there to forgive and help us through the consequences of our sin. He also helps us to learn from our failure, making us stronger as we continue to grow in Him."

"And am I ever glad for that," Mike acknowledged. The others readily agreed.

Brad said, "Would you mind if I share one more quick story before you continue, Mike? I think it'll help reinforce what you've just said."

"Sure!" Mike wiped his brow as though grateful for a reprieve from the hot seat.

"Thanks. It has to do with this process of renewing our minds. I've done some reading about how the brain works, and I'm absolutely convinced that God has created our brains with the capacity to actually rewire themselves, little by little. For instance, the electrical impulses that carry messages from one part of the brain to another travel along pathways—like little highways. Well, you know what happens if you travel the same way to work every day; you could almost drive that route in your sleep."

"Sometimes I *do* drive to work in my sleep," said Vicki.

"Then you know how easy it is to get in a rut. What happens when, one day, you remind yourself that you need to take a different route to work so you can drop off something on the way? Have you ever forgotten to take the new path because you were so used to the old one that you drove right past your turn?

"In the research I've studied, it appears that our brains are like that. Neural pathways are electrically 'dug into' our gray matter, so to speak, so that certain behaviors become routine. However, in victims of head injuries, and in those who have had to have certain portions of their brains literally cut out because of a tumor, it has become apparent that other parts of the brain take over. The electrical impulses literally find a new route to get where they need to go."

"That's incredible," said Kaycee.

"Fearfully and wonderfully made, honey," Sandi said.

"In one unusual case, a young lady who had referred to herself as a lesbian had a car accident. She had some loss of brain tissue from a head injury and some memory loss. Remarkably, she regained all her motor skills, all her speech, and many of her former behaviors that had been part of her personality. But she had absolutely no recollection of being a lesbian—and no urges in that direction."

"I've seen patients like that on my floor," Sandi said. "We had this one lady who used to smoke three packs a day, and then after her accident, she couldn't even remember having smoked before. In fact, after her recovery she couldn't stand the smell of smoke."

"Good example, Sandi. Because we are so fearfully and wonderfully made by our Creator, I truly believe that with each Spirit-led choice we make, our body adjusts slightly—even chemically. That means each time we choose a Spirit-led thought over a lie of Satan, our brain changes ever so slightly. As we make dozens of right choices, and then hundreds, our brain is actually rerouting itself so that the decisions become easier and easier. It becomes an ingrained pattern, and pretty soon, we are quite literally—even *chemically*—different from what we were before.

"So when God tells us in His Word that we are made into 'new creations' in Christ Jesus, I believe it! He recreates us into His image in a more literal sense than we might have previously thought."

Ron stopped writing for a moment and asked, "So you're saying that our behaviors affect our physiology?"

"That's exactly what I'm saying," Brad said. "I have seen patients with post-traumatic stress disorder make remarkable recovery when they start walking in the Spirit. They are able to put their past trauma behind them and start living life as a totally new creature in Christ. Now, obviously, that doesn't happen overnight. In some cases it has required some serious counseling, and it doesn't happen with everyone. But there are enough transformed people walking around as living proof that a Spirit-controlled life results in a far better person than the one who was walking in the flesh before."

"That's really encouraging," Mike said, "because I'm hoping my struggle won't last forever. I'm hoping the more I 'look at the bricks' in my brick pile, the easier it will become to deal with my urges."

"I'm confident it *will* get easier over time, Mike. And remember that this thing called 'walking in the Spirit' is a process. That's why it's often referred to as a daily walk. But God promised that He, the one who began this good work in us, will be faithful to complete it. We just need to be obedient as His Holy Spirit guides us."

"Hey, that's one of the verses in my brick pile," Vicki said.

"And it's a good one," Brad affirmed. "Mike, I'm just curious, what bricks have *you* been looking at when you start to recognize lustful urges?"

"Um," Mike thought for a moment. "That verse we discussed at our last meeting has been a good one. I've been trying to memorize it. I've got it here, inside my Bible. Philippians 4:8: 'Whatever is true, whatever is noble, whatever is right, whatever is pure, whatever is lovely, whatever is admirable—if anything is excellent or praiseworthy—think about such things.'"

Heads nodded all around. It appeared that just about everyone in the group had claimed this verse.

"Great verse," Tom said. "Have you found some positive pictures you can think of when you start thinking of things that are pure and noble and right?"

"Yeah, Tom, I actually have. I start thinking of Jesus, walking around and helping people and doing what is right, pure, noble, and all of those good things. I figure since He was young and single and virile, He must have had the same kind of temptations—and yet He was able to remain pure."

"Good point," Brad said. "Jesus seemed to know how to redirect Himself and His thoughts to the things His Father wanted Him to think about and do. Jesus knew how to use God's Word to take captive every thought and defeat Satan at his game."

"Yeah," Mike said. "I received a funny story from someone in an e-mail. It helps me stay away from the wrong kind of movies, Web sites, or magazines that might tempt me beyond my ability to stay strong. It's about a dad who didn't want his kids to go to certain movies because they contained too much sex and violence. The kids kept begging him, 'But Dad, there's only a little bit—and you hardly notice it's there.'

"Well, this dad decided to teach his kids a lesson, so he baked some brownies—"

"Ooh, brownies, I like this story already," Sandi interrupted.

"I knew you would." Mike laughed. "But just you wait. So the dad baked these brownies, and when his kids got home from school he said, 'Want some of my special brownies? They've got a secret ingredient.' The kids asked, 'What's the secret ingredient?' And the dad answered, 'Dog poop.'"

Sandi cracked up. "Dog poop! Oh my goodness. I don't think I'm hungry anymore."

"Well, the kids said, 'No way, Dad! We're not eating *those* things!' Their father replied, 'Yeah, but there's only a *little* bit of dog poop in the brownies, and you'll hardly even notice that it's there.'

"The dad told the kids that the movies they wanted to see were like his brownies. It might not seem like much, but even a little bit of something bad will make us sick. And we shouldn't be feeding our minds with that kind of stuff either. Even a *little bit* will sicken our minds."

Sandi asked, "Did the kids quit asking to go to those movies?"

"Nope. You know kids. But whenever they would ask again, their dad would simply say, 'Want some of my brownies?'"

Everyone laughed.

"But really," Mike continued, "there's a serious point to that. I guess I was learning that when I am tempted to look at stuff I shouldn't be looking at—whether it's a movie, or something on the Internet, or whatever—I have to remember Philippians 4:8 and allow the Spirit to turn my thoughts away from the dog poop…to things that are true, noble, right, and pure."

Sandi clapped her hands. "I'm gonna tell my kids that one tomorrow. I might even bake 'em some brownies the next time they ask me if they can go to an R-rated movie."

Brad observed, "That really *is* good, Mike, that you've realized you need to use your will to make the right choices and stay away from the stuff that just adds fuel to the fire of those negative urges. Let me ask, too, do you have any strong, Christian, male friends who can act as accountability partners with you? Guys you can trust to keep a confidence and who can pray with you about your temptations?"

"Yes, I do," Mike answered. "After we finished this course three weeks ago, I signed up for a men's group at church. There are a couple of mature guys in the group I'm going to be in, and one of the purposes of the group is to give mutual support through the struggles and temptations we all face."

"That's great," Brad said. "In fact, I would encourage *all* of you to surround yourselves with other believers who are walking in the Spirit—friends you can pray with and support. It's amazing how easy it is to slip back into our old habits if we aren't surrounded by support."

They nodded in agreement.

"As we wrap things up here," Brad said, "I think it would be a great idea for Tom to lead us in prayer. And as you do, Tom, you can pray for Ron, who has agreed to start another small group based on this material. Our church is going to advertise it, and Ron's going to lead it at a local restaurant as a Saturday morning study for Christian businessmen."

Vicki said to Ron, "Way to go, buddy! The teacher's pet has become the teacher himself."

Ron grinned and shook his head, embarrassed.

"No," Vicki said, "I'm serious. You'll do a great job."

"Thanks," Ron said.

"Oh wait!" Brad said quickly, taking the group by surprise.

"Would you allow me just one more really quick story, before we close in prayer?"

"Of course," said Tom.

"It's one my pastor told about a year ago, and it was so good I've shared it with several groups since. It illustrates how God feels about us even though we come to Him with imperfections. That's something I think we need to understand—that no matter how much we might fail along the way, as long as we're making that effort to cooperate with His Spirit and as long as we truly repent each time we fail, He'll be there to accept and forgive us—and help us on toward His ultimate perfection, when we finally see Him face to face."

Sandi said, "Forget the story, Brad, what you just said was inspiring enough."

"Sorry, I got a little preachy there. Here's the story. A lady named Mary Ann Bird wrote about how she grew up 'different.' She was born with a cleft palate.

"You know what it can feel like to be different, don't you?" Brad asked the group. They all nodded. "Well, Mary Ann said she hated her deformity because the kids at school teased her about her crooked lip, crooked nose, lopsided teeth, and nasal, garbled speech.

"When other kids asked her what had happened to her face, Mary Ann would tell them, 'I fell on some glass,' because she figured it would sound better than the truth. She said she was convinced that nobody—except perhaps her immediate family—could ever really love her."

Kaycee was already reaching for a tissue.

"When Mary Ann reached second grade, the school performed its annual hearing test for the kids. Her teacher, Mrs. Leonard, gave the test to all the class members. Mary Ann described Mrs. Leonard as a 'short, round, happy, and sparkling lady.' During the test, Mrs. Leonard would call each student up to the front near her desk, have them stand against the door and cover one ear, and she would sit at her desk and whisper something. Then the student would have to repeat it back to her. Little Mary Ann knew from the previous year's test that the teacher would whisper something like 'The sky is blue,' or 'Do you have new shoes?'

"Well, Mary Ann stood against the door, covered one ear, and listened for her teacher's words. And God Himself must have placed words in Mrs. Leonard's mouth—words meant just for Mary Ann. Mrs. Leonard spoke just seven words. But they were the seven most important words Mary Ann would ever hear. Mrs. Leonard said—" Brad paused for a moment, causing each group member to hang on the silence.

"'I wish you were my little girl.'"

He stopped, letting the words sink in. At first there was only silence. Then, a couple of muffled sobs. Even Brad choked up a little, athough he had told the story a dozen times before.

"And that, my friends, is how God feels about us. He is our Mrs. Leonard. And each of us is His own Mary Ann. No matter how imperfect we may feel at times, He longs for us to be His child."

The group members were visibly moved. Then Sandi exclaimed, "My goodness, Tom, look at you!"

Tom was wiping his eyes with a tissue Kaycee had handed him. He said, "I just had a Coke-can moment."

Everyone watched him, hoping for an explanation.

Tom said, "So *this* is what grace feels like!"

The group laughed, partly in comic relief from their powerful emotions.

Brad seized the moment. "So with that, I leave you in the Spirit's capable hands. Walk in the Spirit. Pour His truths into your mind and heart. Take captive every thought. And keep looking at those bricks!"

The group smiled and nodded, many of them still dabbing tears. Tom took his cue from Brad and said, "Let's give all of this to the Lord in prayer."

Everyone bowed their heads as Tom prayed:

God, our Father, we're so grateful for all
You've done in our lives.
Thank You for the amazing way You continue to work in
each of us through Your Holy Spirit.
You've shown us just how personally You want to know
each of us and that's truly amazing. Thank You.
Thank You for each of the stories we've heard tonight.
It's incredibly encouraging to see visible evidence that You
are still busy at work, making us into new creatures in
Christ Jesus, one brick at a time.
Help us put into practice what we're
discovering from Your Word.
Help us put on the mind of Christ.
Help us renew our hearts and minds
by feasting on Your Word every day.
We commission and pray for Ron as he leads another group
through these tools of discovery and transformation.
Guide him, Lord. Lead others to the
liberating truths we've been discovering here.
We thank You for Your Spirit, who lives
in each of us and who transforms us.
Thank You for the victories we will win through
Spirit-controlled living. In Jesus' name we pray. Amen.

SUGGESTIONS FOR GROUP USE

Expectations for Group Members

It's always a good idea for any group to agree upon a set of expectations before the first session begins. Here's a suggested list of simple rules for an effective group. Feel free to customize them to fit your group:

Confidentiality. What is said in the group stays in the group. Also, if you feel like sharing something personal but think you might be embarrassed by it later, keep your comments general and seek out a trusted friend or counselor for a one-on-one session later.

Commitment. Each group member commits to showing up for every session and to being prepared. Preparation involves reading the assigned chapter or chapters prior to the discussion, completing any homework assignments, and being ready to participate in group interaction.

Camaraderie. As we saw with Tom's group, friendly teasing is a natural part of group life; we tease people we like. But never allow teasing to become hurtful. Encourage one another. Build one another up. Some groups get carried away with banter to the point that it's hard for the discussion leader to keep them on track. Stay aware of your purpose and don't waste other members' time by constantly drifting from the main point.

Consideration. Be considerate of others in the group. Share the wealth and don't monopolize the discussion. Some groups actually place a game board buzzer or bell in the center of the table or room where they meet. If a group member begins to ramble on too long, other members are allowed to use the buzzer or bell to signal that others want to participate too.

Suggestions for Discussion Leaders

Volunteer readers only. Some people are not comfortable reading in public, even in a small group setting. If you ask for someone to read, simply ask for a volunteer. To draw someone out who hasn't read before, you might ask, "Is there someone who hasn't read yet who would like to?"

Volunteer pray-ers only. The same principle applies for group prayer. Don't assume that everyone's comfortable leading group prayer aloud. Ask for a volunteer whenever opening or closing a session with prayer.

Closed enrollment. Because of the need for confidentiality, and because many groups tend to dive more deeply into personal issues after they've been together for a few weeks, it's best not to allow newcomers after the first two weeks. A newcomer thrown into the mix late in the game will change the dynamics completely.

Group guide. Your role as a discussion leader is *not* to be the resident expert for the rest of the group. You don't have to provide all the answers. Your job is simply to help guide the rest of the group in a satisfying, discovery-oriented, learning experience. Resist the urge to answer every question or offer your opinion about everyone else's answers. Allow them to wrestle with issues, dig for their own answers, and come up with their own insights. Allow the Spirit of truth to guide each group member into truth. Don't play the Holy Spirit for your group. He does a fine job all by Himself.

Assistance. Be prepared to provide help. You may find that someone in your group is hurting and needs additional help. Before you start your group, find a professional Christian counselor or pastor who will be "on call" and ready to assist. Then you can gently refer any group member who needs additional help to the person you've lined up. You might even say, at the introductory session, "If at any time you would like to speak to a professional, we have one available to assist. I can give you their number now, and if you need to call after any of our sessions, they are aware that some may be calling."

Disclaimer. If you are not a professional counselor, tell the group up front. Because this book is written for "normal" people and is designed to be taught by nonprofessionals, it's a wise idea to put a disclaimer at the beginning of your course. You can say, "I'm not a professional counselor, but I will be happy to refer you to one should questions come up that I can't answer." You might even want to bring in a professional as a "guest speaker" sometime during your course, as Tom did with Brad.

Celebration. Celebrate your group's accomplishments. Affirm the insights, discoveries, and progress of your group members. Some are hesitant to open up about themselves. Knowing that you are proud of them for doing so will ease their anxiety.

Closure. Finish the course with a celebration such as the testimonial "reunion" in part two of the book. This meeting should happen soon after the course ends, since people's schedules easily take them separate ways. Such a meeting will allow you to:

(1) Bring closure to the group experience. Groups that fizzle don't sizzle. You *don't* want group members feeling like they fizzled. You *do* want them to finish with a bang.

(2) Celebrate what God has done in their lives through the course. Hearing the stories from each group member points to the power of God at work through His Holy Spirit.

(3) Look to see if there's a need to start another group. Maybe your group has a "Ron" in it—someone who will want to lead a new group and "share the wealth."

Dear Reader,

I'd like to hear from you!

I'm always looking for ways to make a good thing better. You can help answer my question: "How can I improve the learning process as it is offered in this book?" If you have an idea that will help me do that, I'd love to hear it.

Also, I'd *love* to hear from you if God has used this book to make a difference in your life or in the life of your small group or church. Joe Serafin and I offer seminars based on the information in this book, and your true story will help us make those presentations come alive. And, with your permission, your story just might wind up in future editions of this book as we encourage other readers with true testimonies of Spirit-controlled living.

If you have a suggestion or story to share, please send it (along with your mailing address and a phone number or e-mail address) to:

Spirit-Controlled Living Stories
c/o Multnomah Publishers
P.O. Box 1720
Sisters, OR 97759

Don't hesitate to share your story. It will be a great encouragement to me, to Joe Serafin, and to the ministry-minded people at Multnomah Publishers.

Yours for Spirit-controlled living,
Clark Cothern

P.S. To book a Spirit-Controlled Living seminar, contact:

Joseph Serafin
Integrity Counseling
517–423–5348

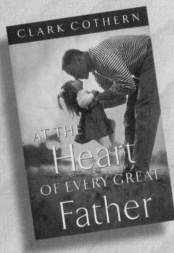
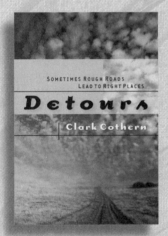